Looking at Art and Artifacts

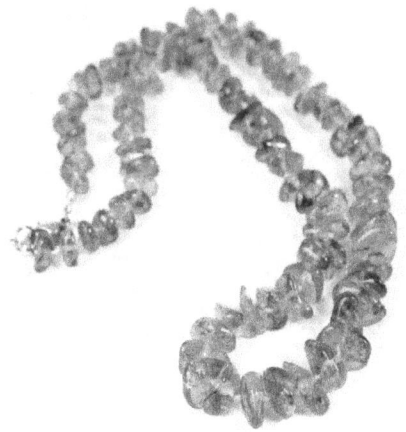

by
David Cycleback

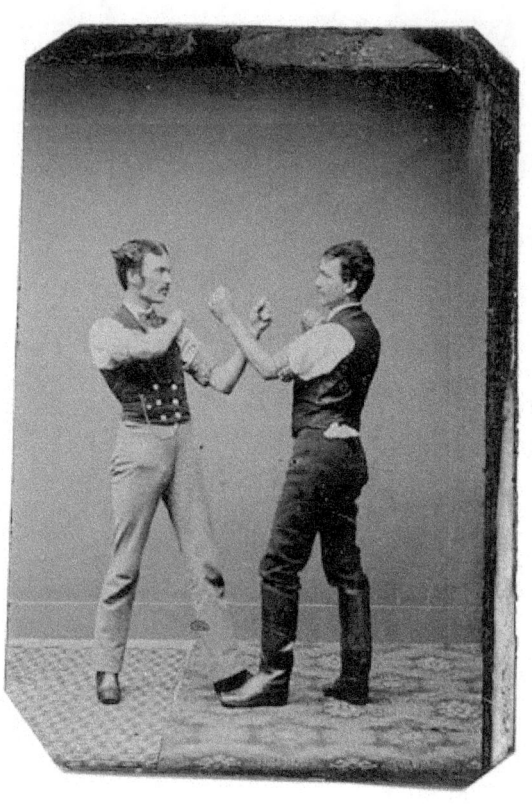

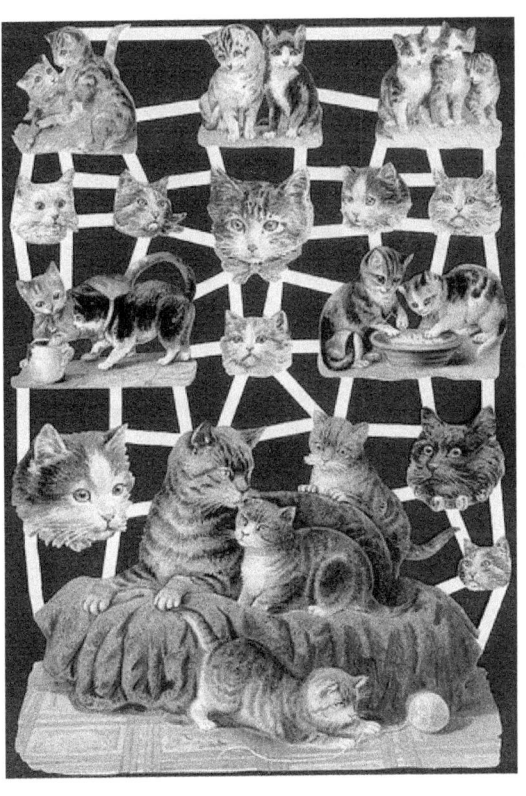

Looking at Art and Artifacts
by David Cycleback

Hamerweit Books
ISBN: 978-1-304-34402-1

(The front cover shows a 1480s tempera painting by
Sandro Botticelli and the back cover shows uranium
glass earrings under ultraviolet light)

Egg Photos

Did you know that most 1800s paper photographs are made out of eggs? Photographic prints require a clear substance to both hold the photochemicals to the paper and allow the chemicals to react, or develop, under sunlight. 1800s photographers found that albumen, or egg whites, worked best. Photo paper manufacturers often had chicken farms on site to supply the eggs. The standard 1800s paper photograph is called the albumen photograph.

A later invention named gelatin worked better than albumen, and most 1900s black and white photographs are called gelatin-silver photos.

Ancient Wax Painting

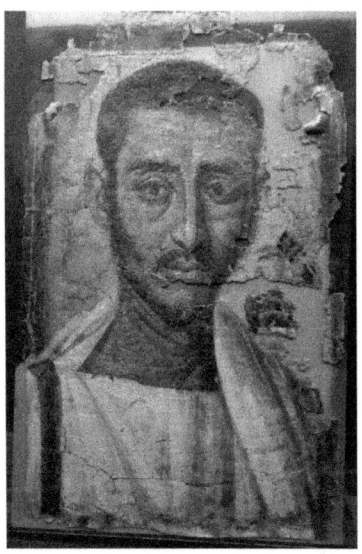

Encaustic painting is an ancient wax-based painting technique that has been revived in recent years.

Using hot bees wax as the material to hold the color pigments, an encaustic painting is easy to identify at a museum or gallery because it has a distinct waxy appearance and sometimes even smell. It was used by the ancient Greeks and Egyptians, with the picture here showing an ancient Greek encaustic painting. Encaustic was rarely used for hundreds of years after due to the universal popularity of oil paints. However, the technique was revived in the 20th century and you can likely find a local beginner's class on how to make your own encaustic paintings.

Science in Art Authentication

In art, science can identify fakes and forgeries, but has limitations in authenticating a work. For example, if a chemist shows that the paint and canvas used for an advertised '1660s Rembrandt oil painting' is from the 1800s, that proves beyond a doubt that the painting is a fake. However, if science shows the canvas and paint is from the 1660s, that doesn't prove the painting is by Rembrandt. It could have been by a student or admirer of Rembrandt copying his style. The chemist's finding is clearly useful towards determining a Rembrandt's authenticity, but the authentication also requires art historians' assessment of the painting's style, quality and other non-scientific aspects.

Dating Paintings by Dendrology

Dendrology, or the study of trees, has been used by art historians to help date many ancient paintings. Before canvas, paintings were most commonly painted on panels of wood, and are called panel paintings. Studying the rings in the wood and knowing when certain regional historical conditions like drought caused abnormal rings, historians are often able to determine the age of the wood for a painting. With the advent of this technique, historians have sometimes found that famous paintings in museums have long been misdated.

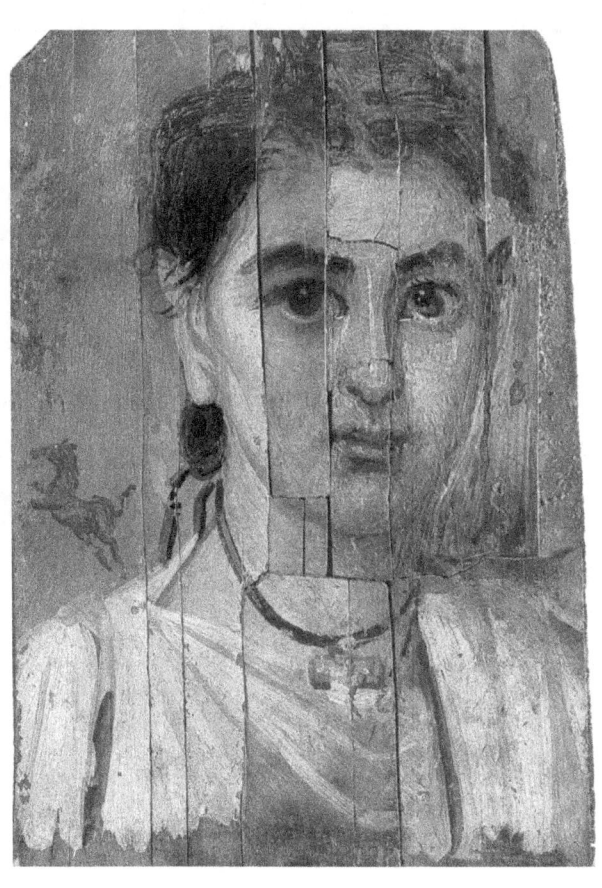

2nd century Egyptian painting on wood panels

What is the value of an artwork that can't be sold or bought?

The kids of a wealthy American art dealer inherited an important artwork by famous American painter Robert Rauschenberg. However, as the work, titled Canyon, incorporated a stuffed federally protected Bald Eagle, the heirs would be committing a felony by selling it. The dealer was only allowed to own the painting due to special permission from the US Government, testimony from Rauschenberg that the stuffed eagle dated to long before the 1940 bald eagle law and upon the promise that the artwork be displayed publicly. It is shown at Metropolitan Museum of Art in New York

As the work could not be sold, the owners' appraisers and Christies auction house appraised its market value as zero. The philosophy being that the value was what it would sell for on the market, and if it could not be sold it had no market value.

The Internal Revenue Service took a different view. It has a board of art experts that appraises art for tax purposes, and they valued the painting as having a worth of $65 million. The IRS accepted the valuation and told the painting's owners to pay $29.2 million in taxes!

It is important to note that the IRS' board of experts said they calculated the $65 million value by comparing it to the sales prices of similar items on the market and did not take into consideration any laws that would prevent it from being sold. Also, one of the experts said that, even with the law, it didn't make any sense to her to valuate it at $0.

The question is what do you think is the value of this artwork?

❧

The story behind a forgery

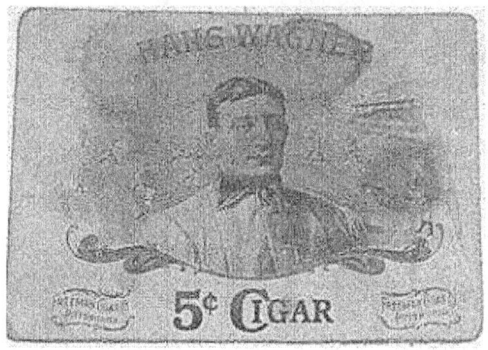

From time to time, one sees offered for sale or auction this Freeman Cigar Co. card depicting the legendary early 20th century baseball short stop Honus 'Hans' Wagner. If offered as vintage, as it nearly always is, it is a fake. The card was made in the 1990s. It has a computer printed image on paper, pasted to cardboard stock.

There are authentic early 1900s Hans Wagner tobacco labels printed on snow white paper intended to be stuck onto tobacco boxes. The labels are extremely rare, with just a few examples known to exist, and come in various designs. The most expensive examples will most likely be offered by major auction houses or top dealers. One of the labels has a close design to this card.

About 1993, a manufacturer of collectable tin signs made a sign based on the design of the just mentioned tobacco label. This man was selling them as modern collectables, not representing themse as vintage. The sign was not an exact copy of the label. He added the 5 cents sign at the bottom for artistic balance. He also said he used a different text font in parts, as he could not find a modern duplicate of the original font.

A couple of years ago a man in Ohio used a computer printer to reprint the tin signs as the tobacco trade cards-- naturally roughing them up and scuffing the cards to make them appear old. He sold them at flea markets to unsuspecting non-collectors who knew the legend of Honus Wagner and thought they had struck gold.

So, when you see one of these cards for sale, treat it as a modern fantasy card in bad condition-- worth two bucks at very most. If you like the design, you can go out and buy one of the 'original' tin signs.

Identifying Amber

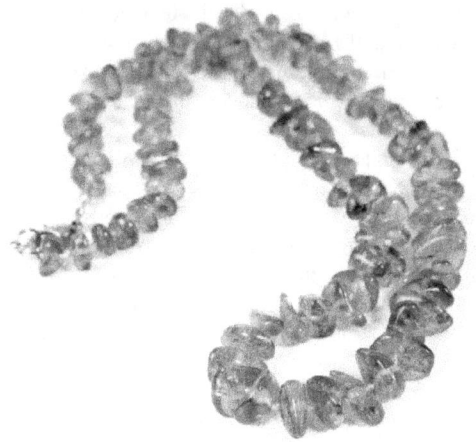

Amber, or fossilized tree resin, is a popular and valuable gem used in jewelry and often displayed.

There are fake amber and other substances that can be mistaken for amber. Amber colored plastics and glass are commonly used to make fake amber. There is also the natural substance called copal that is young amber. Copal is very old, but not fossilized yet and is sometimes passed off as genuine amber.

The following are some quick tips which, in combination, help tell the difference between amber and common imitations. These tests are for bare amber. If amber has metal added, a with a clasp or a ring, it can effect the buoyancy and static electricity tests.

* Amber is warm when you touch it. While plastic is also warm, glass, crystal and mineral gemstones are usually cold. Glass and stones are also heavier

* When rubbed on cloth, even your pants leg, amber becomes electrostatically charged and will attract lint/dust particles and tiny pieces of paper.

* The surfaces of copal and plastics deteriorate when a drop or two of solvent is put on it, but amber is not affected. Plastics are effected by ethyl alcohol and acetone (fingernail polish remover). A few drops of acetone or alcohol put on the surface will reveal if it holds up to the solvent. If the surface becomes tacky or dissolves, it's not amber.

* Amber will float in seawater. Dissolve about 3 tablespoons of salt into per cup of water to test this out. Amber should float and many imitations will sink.

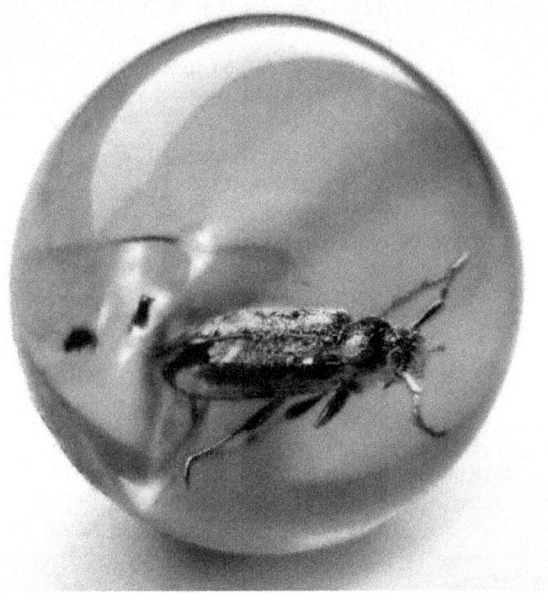

Amber can be found with the remains of ancient insects that got stuck in the tree resin

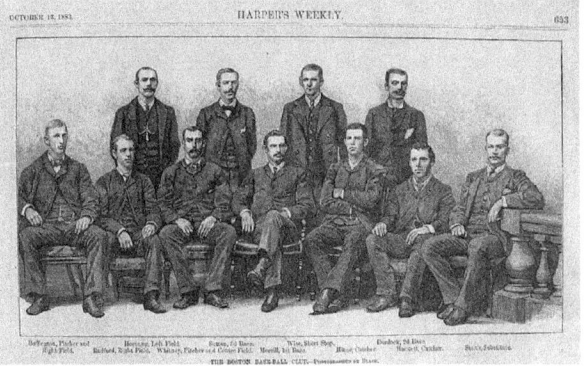

A curious case of dating colors

1800s Harper's Woodcuts, or woodcuts prints from the magazine Harper's Weekly, are popularly collected today. The images show nineteenth century life, including celebrities, sports, US Presidents, war, high society, nature and street life. Though originally black and white, some of the prints have been hand colored over the years. As age is important to collectors, prints that were colored in the 1800s are more valuable than those colored recently. The problem is that modern ideas lead collectors to misdate the coloring.

Due to their ideas about the *old fashioned* Victorian era, most people assume that vintage 1800s coloring will be subtle, soft, pallid and conservative. However, 1800s coloring was typically bright, gaudy, bold and even tacky to modern taste. As Victorian people didn't have color televisions, motion pictures or video games, and were restricted in their travel, they liked their images of exotic places and faraway celebrities to be colored exciting. A learned forger might knowingly use historically incorrect colors, as he knows the average person today would consider authentic colors to be fake.

East versus west

In early Christian culture, the importance was given to the afterlife not life on earth. A result was the early Christian art was not realistic.

On the other hand, early Chinese religions were centered around nature and the early Chinese art had much more focus on and realistic depictions of nature.

Jet Black Jet

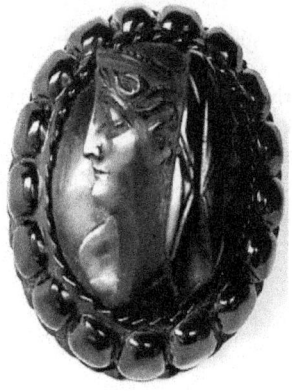

Jet is a black fossilized material prized for its gem-like use in jewelry, including necklaces, brooches, pins and earrings. The term jet black, meaning as black as black can get, comes from jet. When Prince Albert died in 1861, his wife Queen Victoria famously wore jet mourning jewelry and jet was popularly used in general for Victorian era mourning jewelry.

Primarily originating from underneath Whitbey England, jet is fossilized wood, often well over one hundred thousand years old. Though not attractive when it's mined from the ground, it is easily carved and polished to a gem-like black. You can sometimes see patterns from the original tree.

Identifying Genuine Jet. Jet and black glass are sometimes mistaken for each other, but glass is cold to the touch while jet is warm. Jet is light and floats or sinks slowly in water. If you rub jet on unglazed pottery or a sidewalk it will leave a brown/black streak.

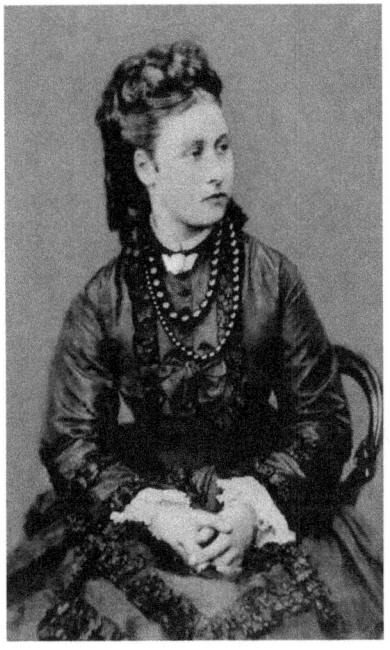

The picture shows one of Victoria's daughters, Princess Louise, wearing a jet bead necklace.

Each art medium is limited in what it can show literally. A painting or sketch doesn't have physical depth or movement. A silent movie doesn't have voices even when the people on screen converse. The letters of a novel can't graphically show a sunrise.

This means a medium must use artificial devices to communicate the literally undepictable.

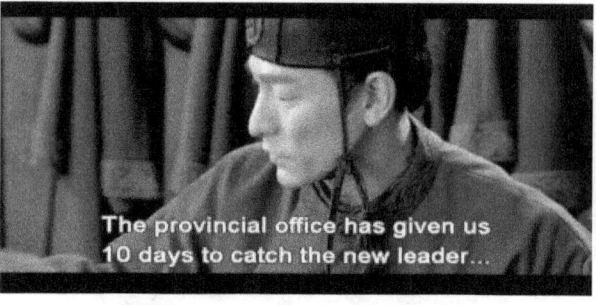

The provincial office has given us 10 days to catch the new leader...

subtitles so viewers know what is being said

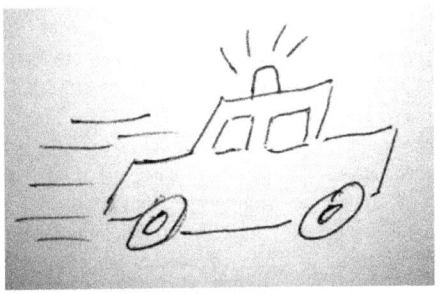

Movement and flashing lights can't be literally shown in a sketch, so the artist symbolizes them with lines. Symbols are a common way to overcome a medium's limitations.

Cancellation Proofs

When artists are finished with a limited edition print run, they sometimes intentionally ruin the printing plate to prevent further prints. They may scratch out part of the graphics to make a big X across the printing plate. To prove they've ruined the printing plate and the print is indeed limited, they make one final print from it. This print is often called the cancellation proof and shows the defacing.

**How to Tell if that World Series
or Super Bowl ring is real**

Amongst the most prized and valuable sports memorabilia are the jewel encrusted championship rings given to players in the NFL, MLB and NBA. The wealthy and famous players themselves often say their rings are their most valuable possessions. The problem and confusion for collectors is there are also on the market inexpensive replica rings and salesman's samples which were samples the ring companies use to try and sell the rings to the teams. The disappointed collector can learn that a replica ring is worth a small fraction of the genuine example.

Happily, it is possible for the average collector to judge if a ring is a real one given to a player or team employee. World Series and Super Bowl rings given to players and team employees are identified as genuine as they use real diamonds and precious metals. Salesman samples and other copies will not have real diamonds, silver or gold. A trip to your local jeweler can identify a World Series or Super Bowl ring as real, as the jeweler will have no trouble determining if the diamonds are real. If the ring has been appraised by a reputable jeweler, the appraisal will have already determined if ring has real diamonds and precious metals used.

These rings commonly come with provenance documentation showing they came from the player or team employee. In cases, the ring comes with an letter of authenticity from the player or family.

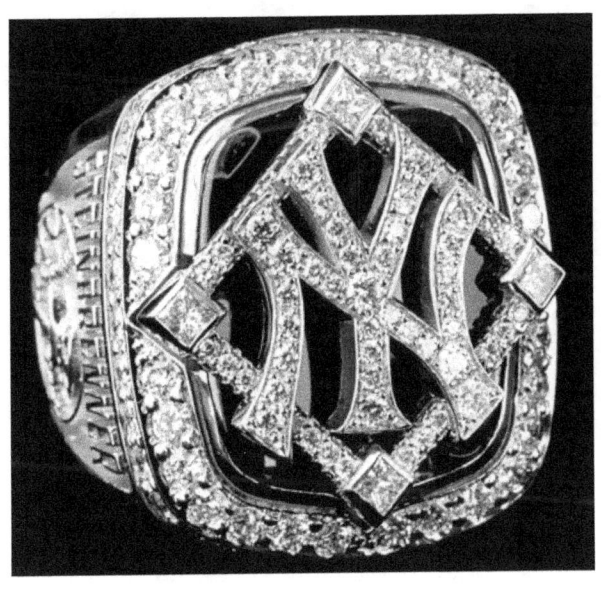

Diamond and gold 2009 New
York Yankees World Series Ring

Press Photos

Press photographs are photographs made by, for or otherwise used by the press and publishing industries. These photos include wirephotos made by wire services like Associated Press and UPI, original photos shot by magazine and newspaper photographers and photos made by Hollywood movie studios and rock music labels to promote their upcoming products to the press.

Press photos are popularly collected, as the images encompass most every popular subject, including sports, movies, music, politics, celebrities, history, space exploration, art, nature and everyday life. Many of the world's most famous photographers have shot press photos, including Ansel Adams, Mathew Brady, Richard Avedon, Alfred Stieglitz, Francesco Scavullo, Carl Horner, Harold Edgerton and Napoleon Sarony. The photos come in a wide range of quality, prices, sizes and styles. Some are large originals with crystal clear and artistic images, while others are small, later generation photos with lesser to poor images.

Most press photos are easily identified due to text on the photo. This text can include a magazine's stamp, a news service's paper tag or a movie studio's terms of use printed below the image of a movie star.

Some photos have an editor's handwritten notes detailing how it was to be used ('Two column picture in Tuesday's Sports Section.') Some photos have production marks showing that it was used in publishing or advertising. Some photos don't have such identifiers, but are known to have come from a newspaper's archives, editor or reporter.

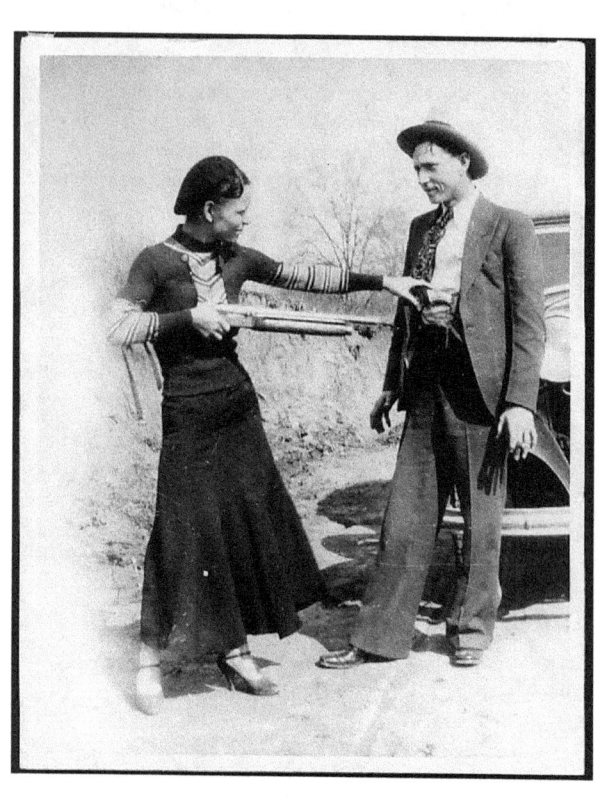

1930s news photo of Bonnie and Clyde

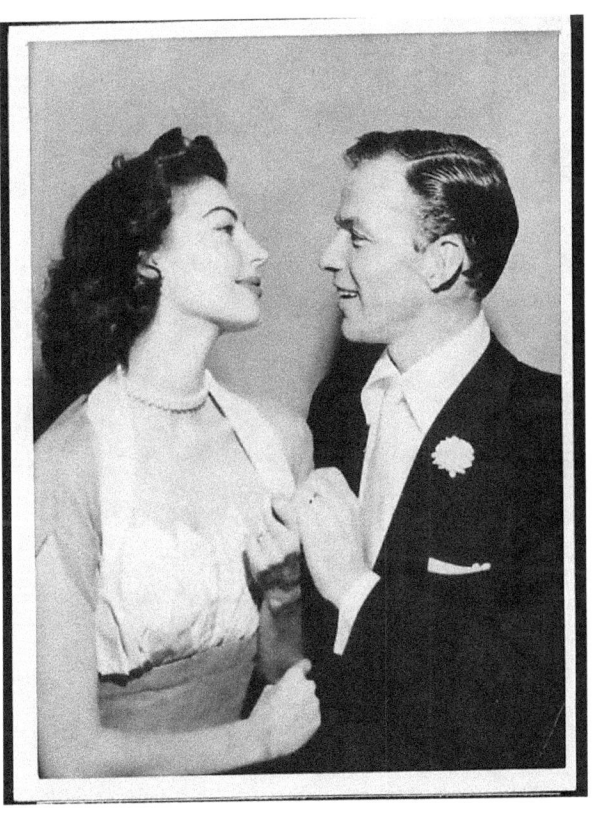

Original news photo of Ava Garner and Frank Sinatra
on their wedding day.

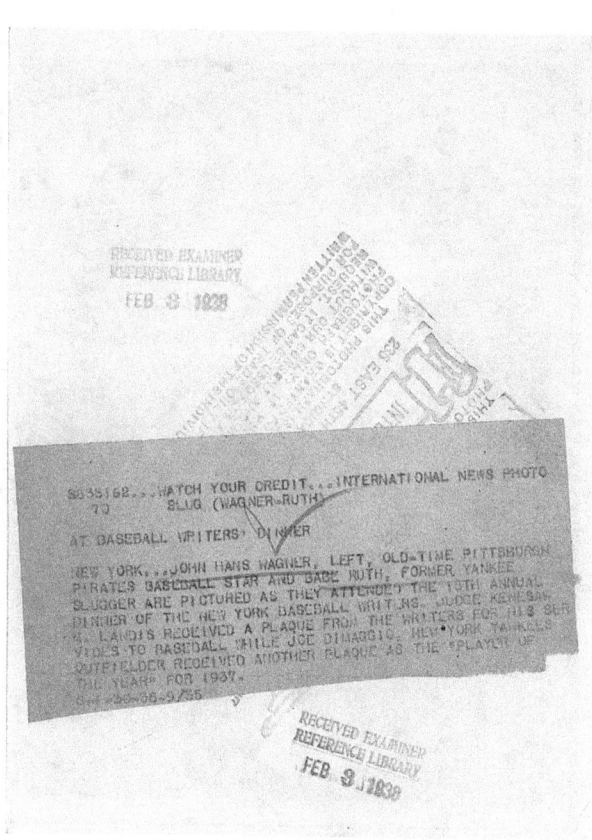

Example of the stamps and paper tags that can appear
on the back of news photos, helping the collector or
dealer to identify and date the photos.

Pastel painting

Pastel is a painting medium where the artists use sticks of pure powdered pigment to draw, instead of brush paint on paper or canvas. A pastel painting can generally resemble oil and acrylic painting, but has a distinct crayon-drawn look.

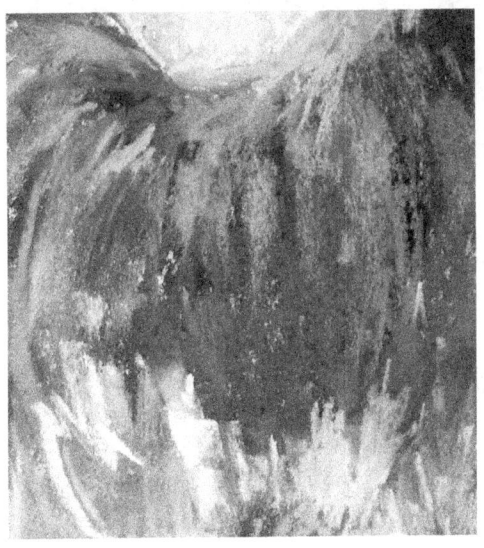

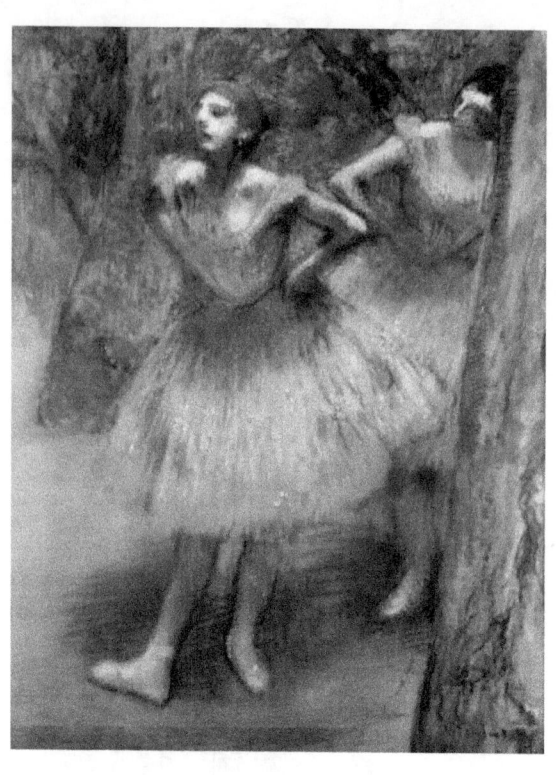

Pastel of a ballerina by Edgar Degas

Radioactive glass

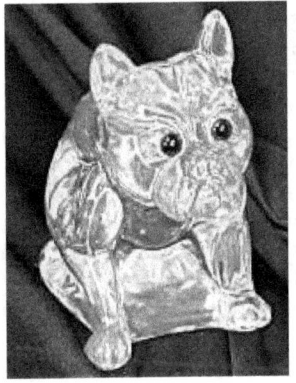

Straight from a 1950s Sci Fi movie!!

Uranium glass is a collectible antique glass that was made with uranium salts. Uranium salts are naturally a bright yellow and they were used to color the glass. Uranium glass ranges from yellow to green, with the green versions having had additional coloring chemicals added. Uranium glass is transparent to opaque and comes in many forms and styles, including plates, glasses, cups and saucers, salt and pepper shakers, candlestick holders and figurines.

As it contains uranium, the glass is radioactive. Happily, the uranium salts added and radiation given off is so low it's considered harmless.

Uranium glass is identified by its general appearance and color (yellow to green) and because the uranium salts makes it fluoresce a bright green under black light. Some advanced collectors and dealers even use a geiger counter to measure the radiation, but for most people a black light is more than enough.

There are sub categories for uranium glass. The problem is different people use the names differently, even sometimes applying them to non-uranium glass that has same superficial appearance. Some areas of the world use the terms differently.

The following are common subcategories.

Vaseline glass is a nickname given to uranium glass that is transparent and with a yellow or yellow-green tinge. It got its nickname as some thought it resembled vaseline. However, some call any kind of uranium glass vaseline glass, some say vaseline glass can only be yellow and some call any kind of transparent yellow glass vaseline glass even if there is no uranium salt content.

Custard glass is a uranium glass that is an opaque or near opaque yellow. Though some call any opaque yellow glass custard glass, even if it contains no uranium.

Jadeite glass is uranium glass that is opaque or semi opaque pale green. However, some call any opaque or semi opaque pale green glass jadeite glass even when it has no uranium content.

With all the competing subcategory definitions, just remember that a black light will tell you if something has uranium salts in it and is genuine uranium glass.

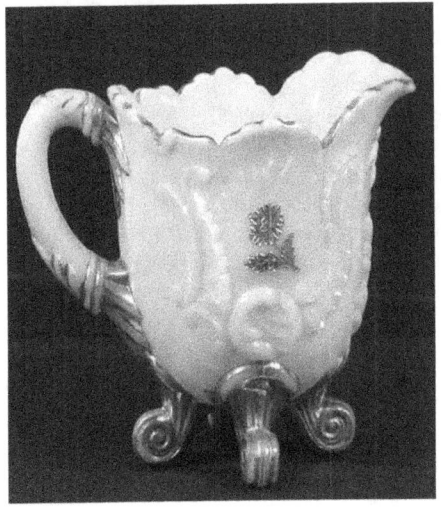

custard glass creamer cup

Microdots

Art, artifacts, collectibles and other valuables are often security marked in case of theft, loss, dispute or later identification. The markers range from overt holograms and stickers to invisible tags allow the marked items to be identified.

An interesting covert marking system uses microdots. Microdots are microscopically small metal discs that have identifying information micro-etched on them. The dots can be the size of standard printed period (.). The etched information can be a serial number that identifies the object's owner. The dots will go completely unnoticed by the average thief, but can be used to trace the item back to the rightful owner.

Microdots and related covert 'shrinking down text' actually is an old time application. German spies used microdots to covertly pass information during WWII

Even as early as the 1870 Franco-Prussian War carrier pigeon messages were photographically shrunk so the bird could carry more text.

microdot

Another covert security marking technology used today is synthetic DNA. Invisible to the naked eye, synthetic DNA is lab made DNA that is identified via lab analysis or with special hand held devices. The synthetic DNA is specially made for the customer, so the DNA on the painting or sculpture identifies the owner.

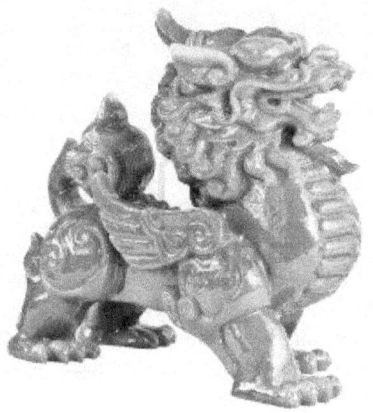

Identifying Jade

To the Ancient Chinese, jade was more valuable than gold and called the stone of heaven. They considered jade to have special powers and symbolic meaning.

Though commonly thought of as green, jade can be found in different colors including white and red, and can be transparent to opaque. Jade is one of two minerals, nephrite and jadeite. Nephrite is the jade the Chinese used, is more common and a touch softer than jadeite. Jadeite is more valuable.

The best way to determine if an item advertised as genuine jade is genuine jade is to take it to a knowledgeable gemologist or geologist. However, the following are some simple tips that will help separate the real from crystal, glass and other faked jade.

** Jade is cold to the touch. Hold it to your face or in your hand It's noticeably colder than glass. Plastic is typically warm.

** Jade is dense and heavy. It has heft in your hand.

** If there are air bubbles in the stone, it is not jade but glass.

** Jade can't be scratched by steel.

** Jade gives a chime-like sound when it's hit by anther stone. Many other stones give a dead thunk. The Chinese made flutes and other instruments from jade.

** Jade often has a shiny, greasy looking surface.

** Jade is usually super smooth. If it feels bumpy when you run your fingernail across is, it's likely not jade.

Interpreting a work of art

When you critique a movie, do you think it important what the director thought the movie was about and what he was trying to do? When you read a book or look at a painting, is it important for you to know the artist's intention? Have you ever made an interpretation of a work of art, later found out what was the artist's and found it different than yours? What was your reaction?

These types of 'which interpretation is correct?' questions touch on topics that have long have been important in aesthetics.

Years ago the prominent literary school of thought was that the most important thing in interpreting and studying a book was the author's intent. This was later rejected, with an influential school of thought entirely dismissing author's intention and saying all that mattered was the reading of the text itself. Part of this rejection was the thought that one can't reliably know the author's intent. Today many scholars find both extremes, well, extreme.

A related school was that a work of literature was a reflection or representation of the author's biography. Others rejected this, in part because artists have imaginations, can make things up.

Another school was that art was judged by the audience's reaction to it. There is some validity to this in that art is a communication, it is intended to communicate ideas to the reader, viewer or listener. Others rejected this idea, saying audience reaction was irrelevant, and a movie shouldn't be judged by the reaction of whichever random audience viewed it. Again, most people today reject the rigidity of both sides. Many think you can't judge art solely by audience reaction, but that it's relevant.

All these views beg the question of is there a correct way to interpret art? Is there even a correct method to determine which way is correct?

Many ancient Egyptian tomb paintings showed what the buried wanted brought with him or her to the afterlife. This included slaves, animals, fruit orchards, buildings. The insides of the tombs often also contained small models of these things. As the tomb buried were royalty, they wanted to continue to live the luxurious life they had lived on earth.

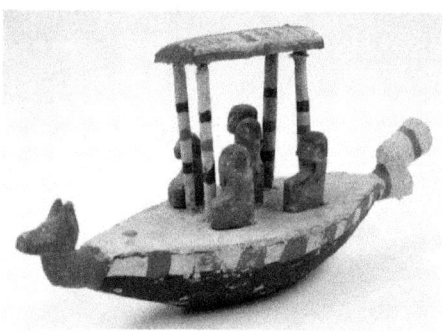

tomb model of a boat and people

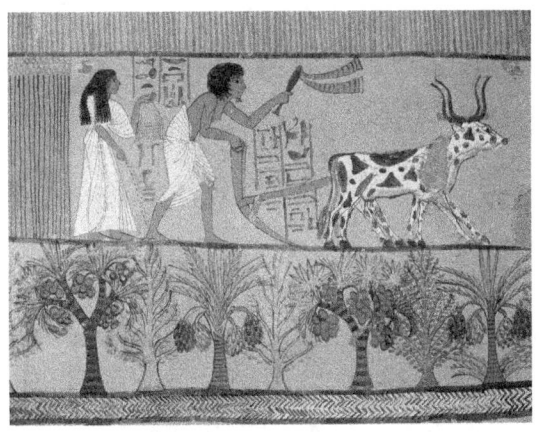

Egyptian tomb painting of farming, slaves and orchard.

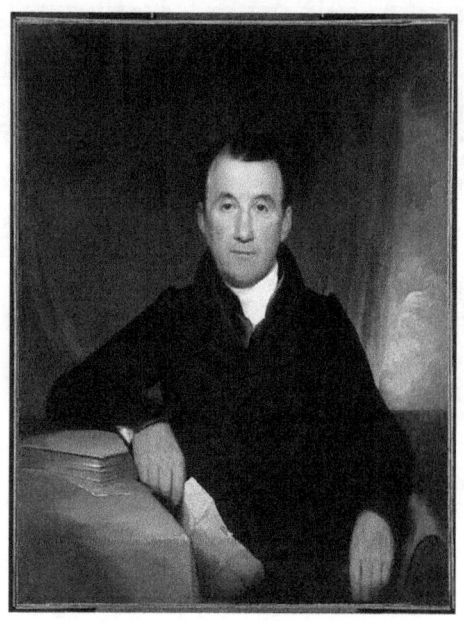

Samuel Morse

Oil painting of Jonas Platt by Samuel Morse

Though Samuel Morse's fame rests with his telegraph system and Morse Code inventions, his vocation was as of professor of painting and sculpture at New York University.

Picasso sometimes wasn't trying to make something that was beautiful, and considered the expected and cliched opinion of whether it was beautiful or ugly irrelevant to the work.

Does art have to be beautiful? Is art defined as art by its beauty?

&

During his day, J.S. Bach's music was considered old fashioned and out of date. 20th century pianist and Bach champion Glenn Gould said Bach was such a genius he wasn't tied to an era, even if that mean going backwards.

Identifying reproduction paintings

Many paintings have been reproduced. Reproductions range from the blatantly obvious to the more deceptive. I assume I don't have to explain to you that the Mona Lisa on your umbrella isn't the original. However reproductions can be more realistic, can be on canvas, framed and even with fake brush strokes. A number of well known artists have had their paintings reproduced. Leroy Neiman and Thomas Kincaid come to mind.

Identifying a reproduction is usually easy, though there might a few bit trickier instances. The following are a few things to look for:

** A fine color dot matrix pattern under high magnification. A photomechanical or digital reproduction of a painting or photograph will translate the original into a fine pattern of different tiny color dots. With strong magnifying glass or microscope examine a magazine photo or picture postcard to see what this dot pattern looks like. A painting is made with brush strokes of solid paint and will not have this maze of dots throughout the image. If you've identified this dot pattern you can stop. It's not a painting. It's a reproduction.

** With an oil or acrylic painting, there will be physically raised brush strokes that you can see and feel. Like a relief map. If you run your finger across the original Mona Lisa or your neighbor's acrylic landscape, you'll feel the brush strokes.

With watercolor and gouache (opaque watercolor) paintings there will be no such raised brush strokes, the surface can feel smooth and the painting can be on regular paper. This makes reproductions of these paintings more deceptive before you take a close look. Happily, that tiny color dots pattern under magnification will always give it away as a reproduction.

In some professional reproductions, clear paint is added over the top of the print to simulate raised brush strokes, but upon examination the fake brush strokes won't match up with the graphics and, looking closely from the side, the coating will be clear. These clear brush strokes are intended more as a superficial coating than anything to deceive. And you should still be able to see the tiny dots pattern through it.

** If a painting is supposed to be an acrylic or oil painting or anything with heavy paint, turn the painting around, put it in front of a light source and see how the image looks from behind. Oil and acrylic paint is an opaque, often thick substance and will block light (of course, then, that's what opaque means). With a real oil or acrylic painting and its heavy paint, some parts of the image you can see while others will be completely blocked out by the paint. Wth a lithograph or digital print on canvas or paper, you should be able to see the whole graphics fine-- as there is no paint to block the light.

*** The real Starry Night doesn't come in calendar form or in 8x10 six packs at Target.

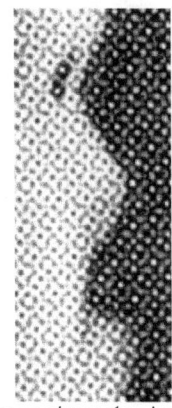

Close up picture showing the dot pattern in a reproduction

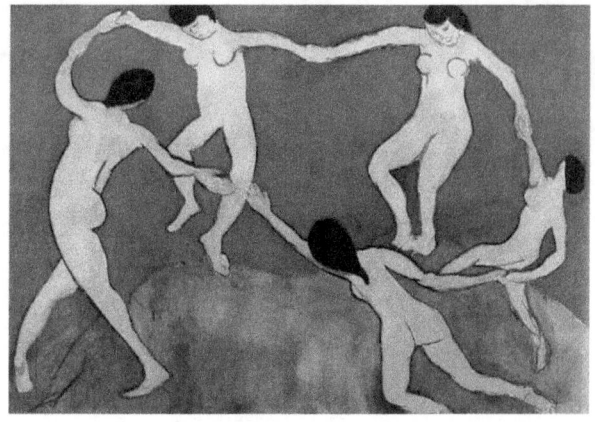

Art as imaginary

What's going on in of a work of art is at least partially made up by the viewer. People perceive the above Chagall design as showing dancing and movement, yet there is is none. The figures are stationary. The movement is a figment of the imagination.

Pewter

The dull silvery metal can be identified because it contains lead and will make a mark like a pencil on paper.

Lewis Carroll as photographer

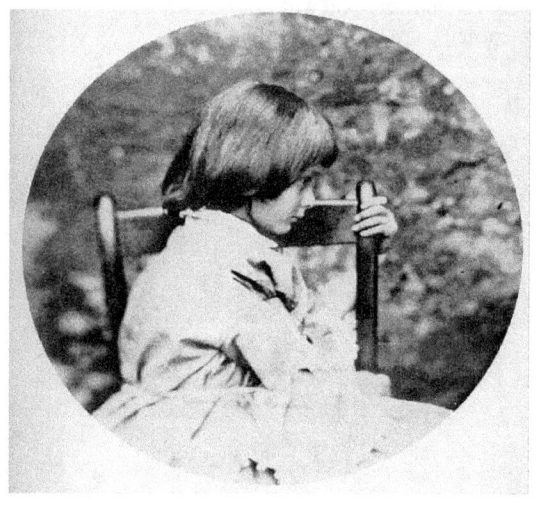

Though famous as a writer of 'Alice and Wonderland' children's books, Oxford mathematics professor and reverend Charles Dodgson (pen name Lewis Carroll) was also an accomplished photographer. He had his photography studio on the Oxford campus. The photo is a Dodgson portrait of Alice Liddell, the young girl who Alice was based on.

The Impossibleness in
Translating Poetry

Beyond the changed words, the foreign
language translation of a poem alters and often
destroys the original poem. With rare exception
the translation of a beautiful poem can be
similarly beautiful or literally faithful, but not
both.

Poetry is uniquely tied to the native
language-- the unique word definition, culture,
diction, rhyme, sound, meter, feel and even
physical length of words and phrases. Due to
the literal and figurative differences between
languages, a foreign language translation of a
poem not only changes the literal words but the
poem. It is not possible to change the language
and perfectly preserve the original meaning.

This is elemental ly illustrated by the
translation of simple rhyming poems. While
'dog' and 'fog' rhyme, the standard Spanish
translations of 'perro' and 'neblina' do not. To
make the translation rhyme, the translator must
take liberties with the literal meaning. To keep
intact the literal meaning, he must omit the
rhyming.

In order to preserve artistic meaning,
many translators consciously dismiss literal
translation. The translation is often as much the

artistic creation of the translator as it is of the original poet.

The reader of a translation is not reading the original poem. The translation may be closely related and beautiful and profound, but it's something different. This illustrates the problem with those who take literally modern translations of ancient texts.

Egg Tempera Paintings

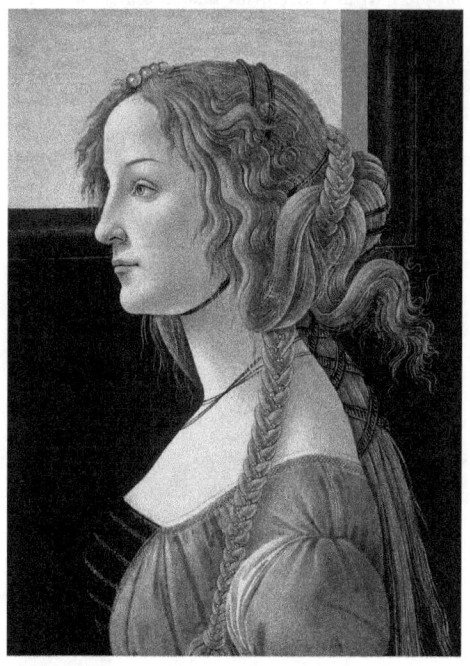

Tempera, often called egg tempera, is an ancient type of paint and painting that pre-dated oil paint in popularity. Many ancient Egyptian and Western Medieval paintings were tempera, and the paintings of Michelangelo and Botticelli are tempera. The wonderfully modern looking tempera shown earlier was painted in the 1400s by Sandro Botticelli. Tempera was the most popular form of painting until the 1500s, when it was replaced by oil paint. Some artists today still paint in tempera. 20th century American Andrew Wyeth is the most famous modern egg tempera painter. The paint usually has the color pigment mixed in egg yolk, thus the name egg tempera.

Due to the distinct paint qualities, tempera has a look and feel much different to oil painting. Tempera paint is thin in consistency and dries very fast. This means the artist painstakingly paints in careful, thin brush strokes and slowly adds up the lines to create the overall detail. When you look closely at a tempera, the graphics are usually made up of thin lines, often overlapping and cross hatching to build up color and detail. These lines mean the painting often closely resembles a color pencil drawing.

There are no big, bold brush strokes and thick globs of color as can appear on oil and acrylic paintings. Tempera paint is never thick on the canvas or board as with oil. Tempera paintings usually have a matte finish, whereas oil paintings tend to be glossy.

Tempera paintings tend to have overall brighter colors and with less contrast in the details. Notice the lack of contrast in the face of the Botticelli painting shown here. The shadows of her skin are lighter and more gradual than the stark dark to light that often appears in oil paintings. The lighter contrast is because the artist created the details and colors by carefully building them up thin overlapping line by thin overlapping line.

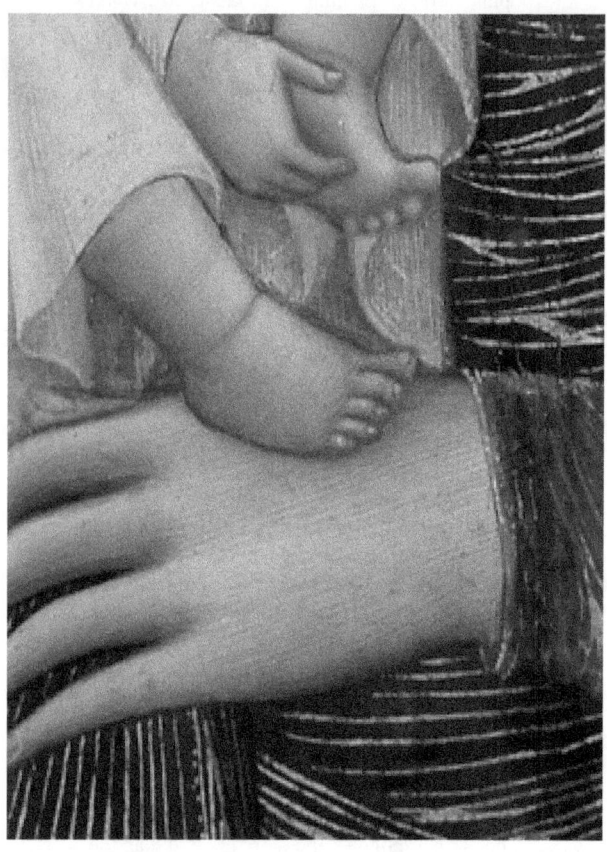

Notice the fine lines in this tempera painting

The Unique Subjective Experience

Subjectivity is a constant and integral part of the human experience. Love, lust, like, dislike, taste, smell, views about beauty and ugliness and art. How you view this paragraph and this book involves subjectivity— your taste about the writing style, word choice, chapter subjects and ordering.

By definition, a subjective experience is a product of the individual's mind. While real and often profound, the subjective experience cannot be objectively measured by others. When someone is listening to music, the music's note, pitch, speed, volume and the listener's ear vibration and heartbeat can be measured by scientific instruments, but the listener's aesthetic experience cannot. This experience is experienced by the listener alone. Even if asked to, the listener could not fully translate the experience to others, in part because it is beyond words.

It's doubtful that two people have the same subjective perceptions. People may have similar, but not identical perceptions. People regularly like the same song but perceive it differently. It's common for best friends to like a movie, but one likes it more than the other or for different reasons.

Cartes de visite

Popular in the mid to later 1800s, cartes de visite, also called CDVs, were business card-sized photographs with a thin paper photo pasted to a larger cardboard backing. They were used for many purposes, including soldier ID cards, family photos, advertising pieces and collectibles. Carte de visite is French for 'visiting card' and many people used them much like business or calling cards.

The cardboard backings come in a variety of colors and designs and usually have the photography studio stamped on the back and/or front. Singular (one photo) is carte de visite, plural (multiple photos) is cartes de visite ('s' added after carte). Most cartes de visite are inexpensive, but rare premium examples can fetch more than $100,000 at auction.

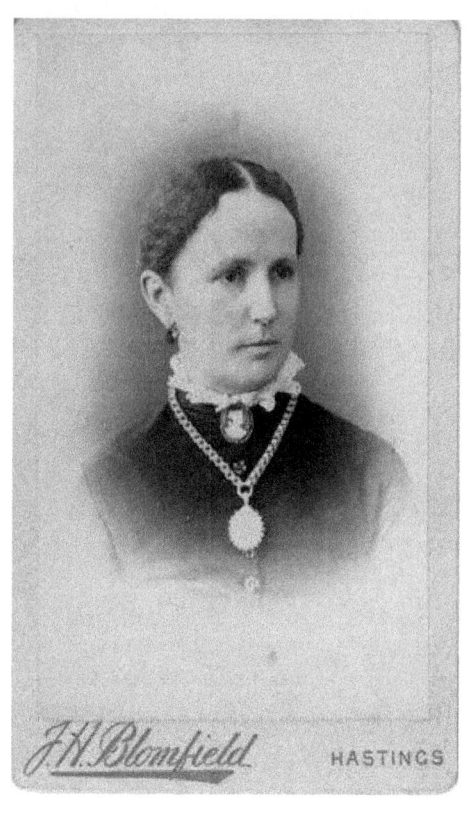

J.H.Blomfield   HASTINGS

1800s carte de visite of woman with
photographer's name and city on the
bottom.

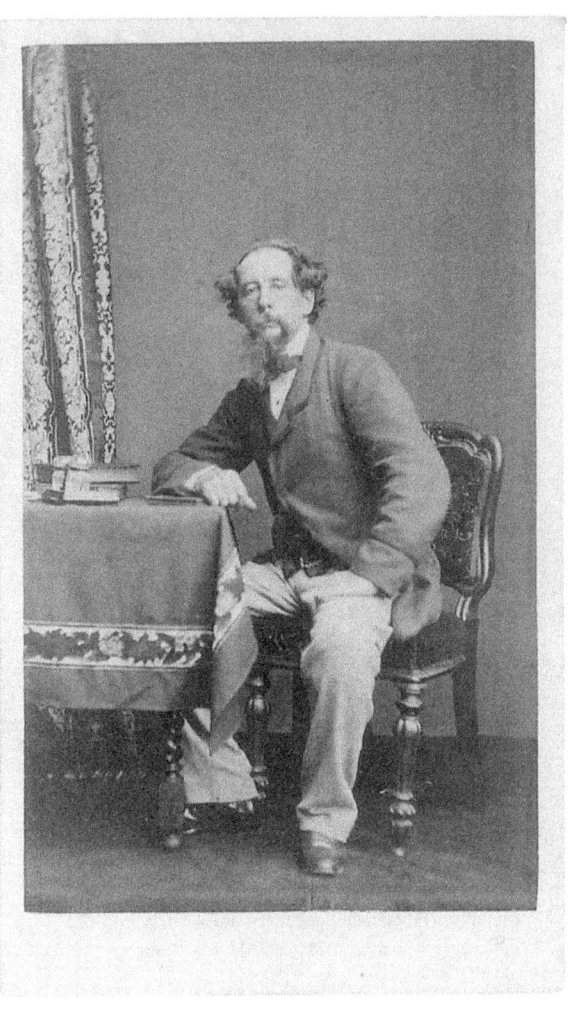

carte de visite of Charles Dickens

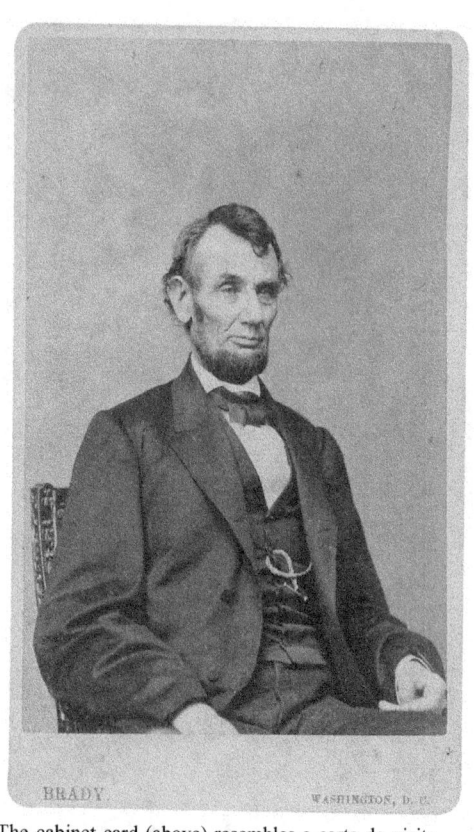

BRADY.   WASHINGTON, D. C.

The cabinet card (above) resembles a carte de visite, except is much larger. It was nicknamed the cabinet card as people liked to display them in cabinets. This cabinet of Abraham Lincoln has the front stamp of famous Civil War photographer Mathew Brady.

**A very basic ceramics
identification guide**

Ceramics (cups, bowls plates, jugs, figures, etc)
are divided into three major categories:
stoneware, earthenware and **porcelain**. This
section is a very quick identification to which of
the three is that figurine in the antique store,
bowl in the estate stale, or coffee cup in your
kitchen cabinet. It is usually easy to make an
identification, though there will always be some
gray areas where it's hard to tell if something
falls into one or the other.

Porcelain, which has that signature refined,
smooth, thin, 'dainty tea cup' look, is the only of
the three categories that is translucent. This
means if you hold up the item to the light you
can see light come through. If you pass your
fingers between the item and the light, you will
see the shadow of your finger pass by.

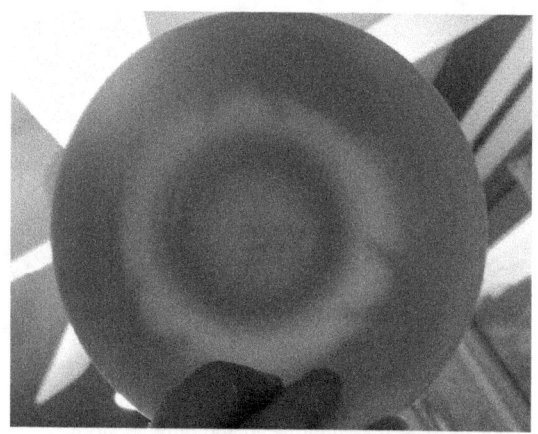

Porcelain cup held to light showing its translucence

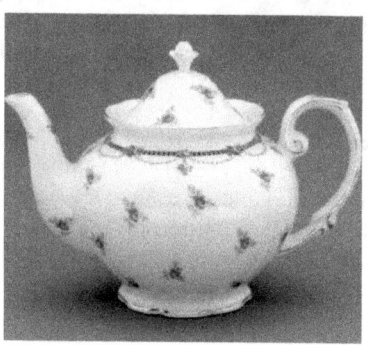

porcelain tea pot

Stoneware, which is opaque (doesn't let through light), tends to be heavy and substantial. It can look more basic, handmade and primitive— like that old time country folk art jug. Anywhere the object is unglazed the clay is darker, usually dark grey but also sometimes light brown, sometimes with specs in it, and has a rough texture, as it if was made out of a chunk of clay in middle school pottery shop. Stoneware cups, bowls, plates and similar usually have unglazed bottoms where you can see the rough, dark material. Due to being fired at a higher temperature, stoneware can hold water even when unglazed—- thus the unglazed bottoms.

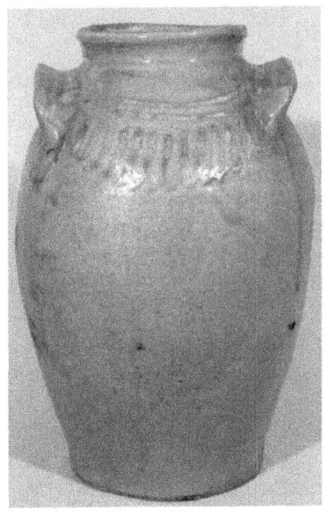

Heavy, folk art look of a stoneware jug

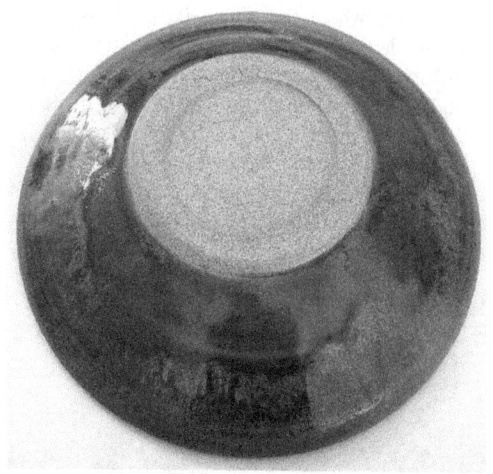
unglazed bottom of a stoneware bowl

Earthenware, which is also opaque, is the most common form of ceramics. Most of your 'department store' dinner plates and coffee cups in your kitchen are earthenware. Unlike stoneware, earthenware is not waterproof when unglazed. This means earthenware is almost always glazed all over, including on the bottom. This is particularly true for a cup, bowl or jug that is intended to hold liquid. On an earthenware cup, plate or bowl the entire item will be glazed except for a thin white or off white rim at the bottom. That part is left unglazed so the item doesn't go sliding across the dinner table. At this unglazed area, or any other glazed area such as a chip, the material is milky or chalky (unlike the coarse dark stoneware material).

Just remember that an earthenware cup, bowl or plate will be glazed on the bottom (except for the chalky rim), while heavy stoneware is unglazed on the bottom and has a darker, rough texture.

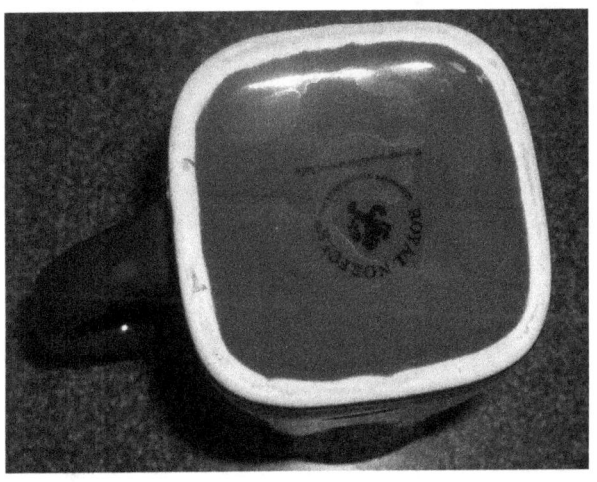

Chalky white rim on the bottom
of earthenware coffee cup

William Blake's unique books

Poet William Blake's 'Illuminated books,' which combined his visionary art and words, were printed, hand bounded and hand colored in watercolor by Blake himself. Blake was a master print maker and, in particular due to the hand coloring, each book is unique.

What authenticity is

In all areas of collecting, from movie memorabilia to oil paintings, something is authentic if its true identity is described accurately and sincerely.

If you pay good money for an "original 1930 Greta Garbo photograph by the famous Hollywood photographer George Hurrell," you expect to receive an original 1930 Greta Garbo photo by George Hurrell. You don't expect a 1970 reprint or a photo by an unknown photographer.

An item does not have to be rare or expensive or old to be authentic. It just has to be accurately and sincerely described. A cheapo 2003 reprint can be authentic if described as a cheapo 2003 reprint.

Errors in the description of an item are considered significant when they significantly affect the financial value or reasonable non-financial expectations of the buyer. An example of the reasonable non-financial expectations would involve a collector who specializes in real photo post cards of her home state of Iowa and makes it crystal clear to the seller that she only wants postcards depicting Iowa. Even if there is no financial issue, she would have reason to be disappointed if the purchased postcard turned out to show Oklahoma or Minnesota.

Many errors in description are minor and have little to no material effect. If that 1930 Greta Garbo photo turns out to be from 1934, it may not affect the financial value or desirability to the purchaser.

The subjectivity of perception

When a human being visually perceives, he mentally organizes, sorts, groups, prioritizes and labels the things in the scene. When you look at an ink sketch, you mentally assemble the ink lines, squiggles and dots into a form. "It's a kitty cat." "It's a cottage in the woods." You decide which ink marks belong together and how, and which do not. Two people can and do group the ink markings differently.

A Rorschach ink blot is perceived differently by different people. The ink blot remains the same. The viewer changes. Rorschach ink blots are used by psychiatrists and psychologists to learn about an individual's mind.

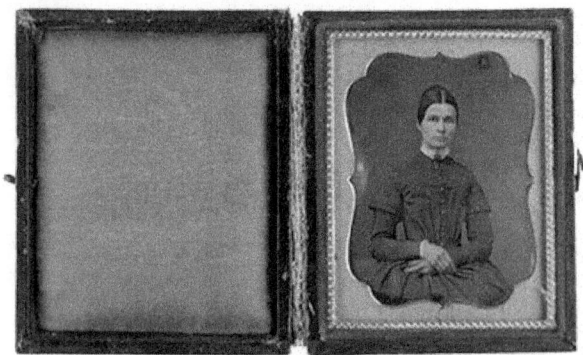

∽

Early Metal and Glass Photos.

Mid 1800s Daguerreotype photo in its case

People are usually surprised to learn that many 1800s photographs were not paper but glass and metal. The most common of these are the Daguerreotype, ambrotype and tintype.

Invented in 1839, the Daguerreotype was the history's first practical photograph and has the image on a copper sheet coated in silver. The image has a magical mirror-like quality and some collectors say it is the most beautiful of all photographs.

Invented several years after, the ambrotype has the image on a pane of glass backed in black.

Invented a few years after the ambrotype, the tintype has the image on a sheet of iron,

78

resembling tin. The tintype was the most popular 'hard' photograph. They were especially popular during the American Civil War. Many families have tintypes of their ancestors.

Daguerreotypes and ambrotypes were usually housed in fancy 'cases,' which resemble miniature ornate books. When the case lid is opened the photograph is ornately matted and framed inside.

Early tintypes were held in cases, but in later years in custom made cards, display envelopes and albums. The cards, envelopes and albums were specially designed to hold and attractively display the tintypes. Tintypes from the later 1800s are also often found au natural, meaning not held in anything.

These early metal and glass photographs are small by today's standards, but come in many sizes. Metal and glass plates were manufactured then sold to the photographer or photography studio. The photographer could use the entire plate to make a large photograph, or, as was more common, cut up the plate to make multiple smaller photographs. As a result, most tintypes and Daguerreotypes have irregular cuts including crooked edges and clipped corners.

Other more obscure early 'hard' photographs include the orotone (glass backed in gold, giving a golden tone, usually framed), the opaltype (white glass, often hand colored), ivorytype (on faux-ivory and often hand painted to resemble a little painting) and the autochrome (glass, the first color photograph).

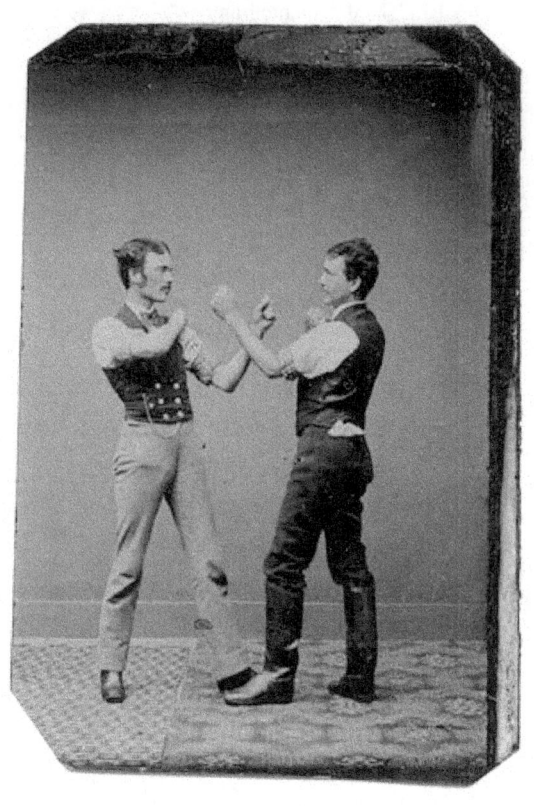

Late 1800s tintype showing boxers posing in the photography studio. This shows how metal pates are often unevenly cut and with clipped corners,

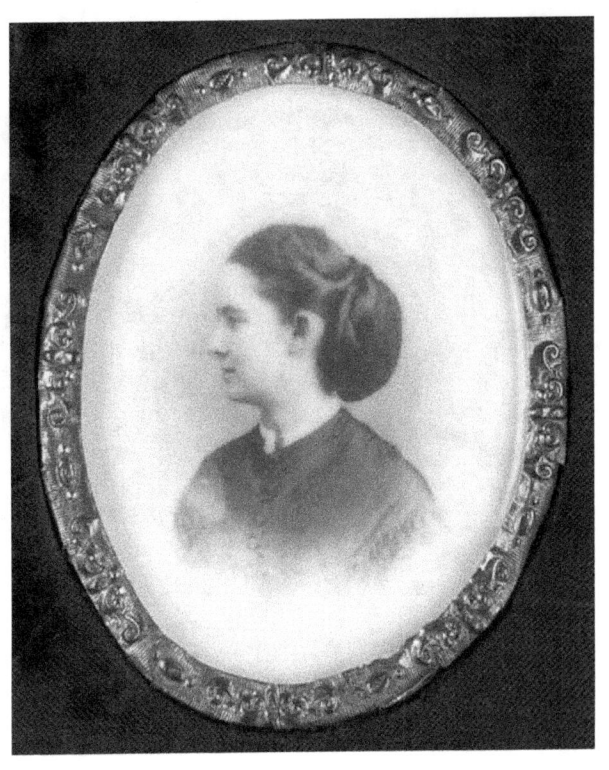

1800s opalotype in a tinfoil frame. The image is on
white glass, giving it a milky appearance.

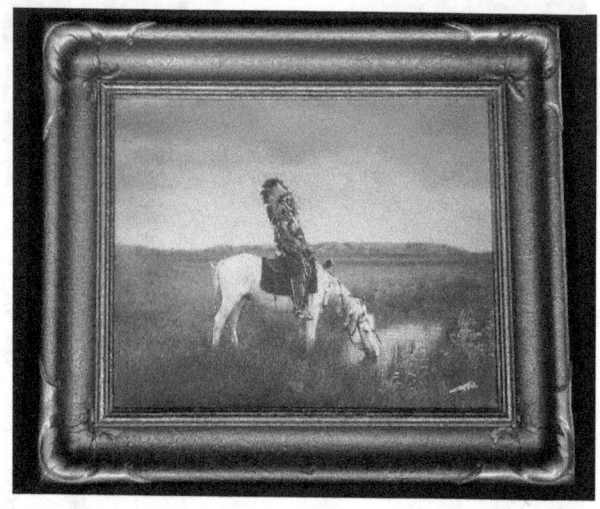

Turn of the 20th century orotone by Edward Curtis, famed documenter of American Indian life. The photo has a golden tone and is in the original leather frame.

❦

The most expensive sports autograph

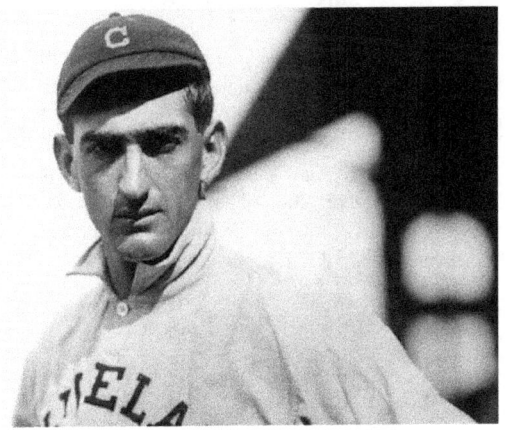

Though to non-fans he's not a household name like Babe Ruth and Joe DiMaggio, Joe Jackson has near mythical status to fans and collectors of early baseball. An illiterate from South Carolina, Jackson was one of the great hitters of the day before being banned for life for his participation in the fixing of the 1919 World Series. As he could barely write his name and usually had his wife sign for him, his signatures are ultra rare and the most expensive sports autograph on the market. A signed baseball will sell for tens of thousands of dollars.

Silver pocket change

United States nickels, dimes, quarters, half dollars and dollar coins dated 1964 and earlier are 90 percent silver.

There is an ultra rare and valuable 1965 silver US dime that is in part identified by its completely silver edge. The normal non-silver 1965 dimes have a visually noticeable brown/copper colored layer on the edge.

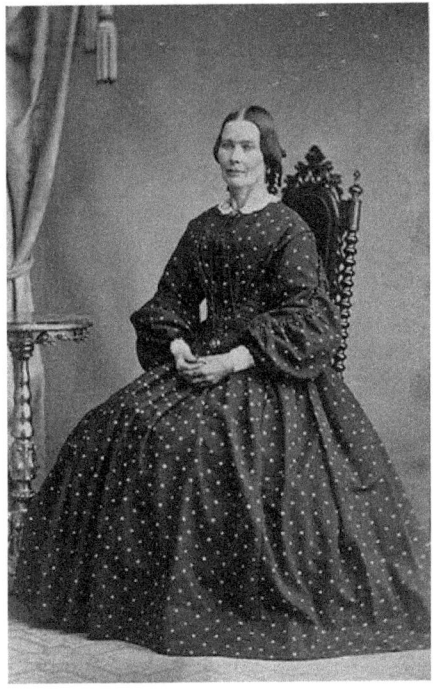

Why all the sour faces?

An often asked question is why don't people in old photos ever smile? The answer is early photography was primitive and the camera's shutter had to be left open a good while to take the photo. Back then, there was no such thing as

85

an instantaneous snap shot. The subjects had to stay perfectly still during the time the shutter was open or the image would come out blurry. This means they rarely smiled, were usually sitting in a chair or standing while leaning against something like a wall, book shelf or table.

Early photography studios sometimes used wooden stands and braces designed to hold still a person who was standing. If you look at the American Civil War image on the next page, you can see the base of the braces holding still the two soldiers.

Away from the photography studio, nineteenth century people likely smiled, laughed and joked around as much as we do.

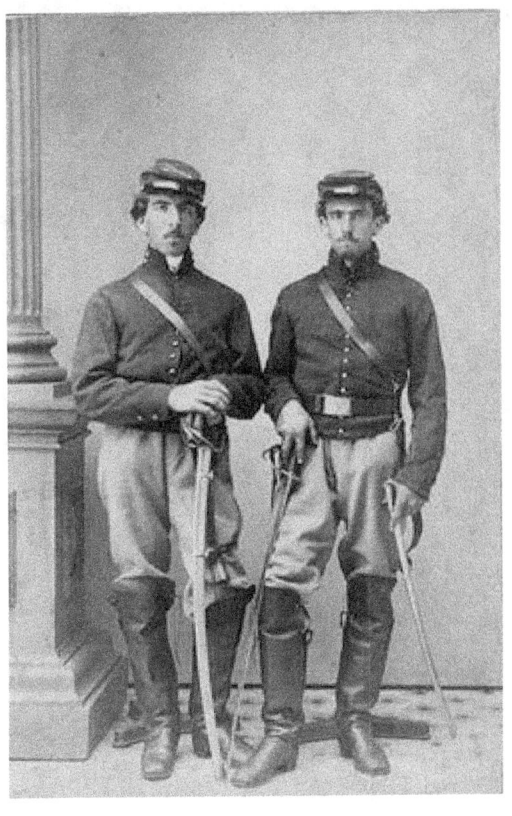

Behind the American Civil War soldiers you can see
the base of the wooden stands used hold them
motionless.

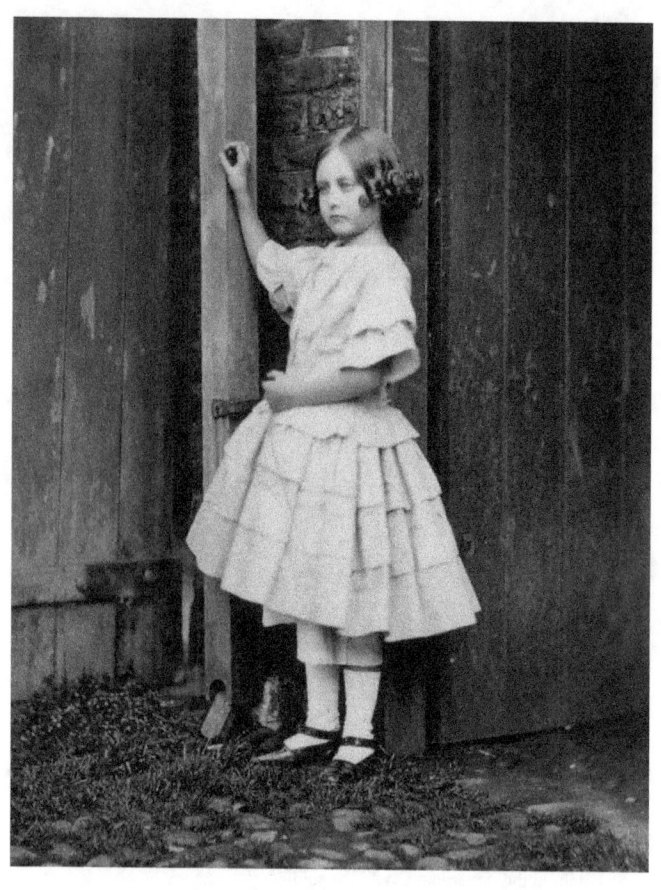

Notice how the girl is resting her back against the
door frame and her hand against the beam.

Victorian scraps

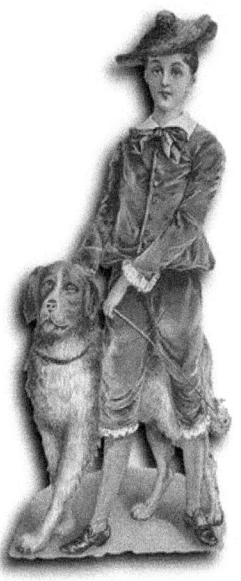

A popular hobby in the 1800s was collecting 'scraps.' Scraps were small factory manufactured paper pieces depicting most every popular subject from cute animals to royalty, soldiers to flowers. They were nicknamed scraps because they resembled scraps of paper. They were sold to collectors in uncut sheets. With early sheets, the individual scraps had to be cut out by hand. The pieces in the later sheets came factory die cut. The later versions were brightly colored, detailed and often embossed.

Scraps were initially used to decorate cakes in early 1800s Germany. By the late 1800s, they were typically collected and pasted into albums with trading cards, greeting cards, cut out pictures and other colorful ephemera.

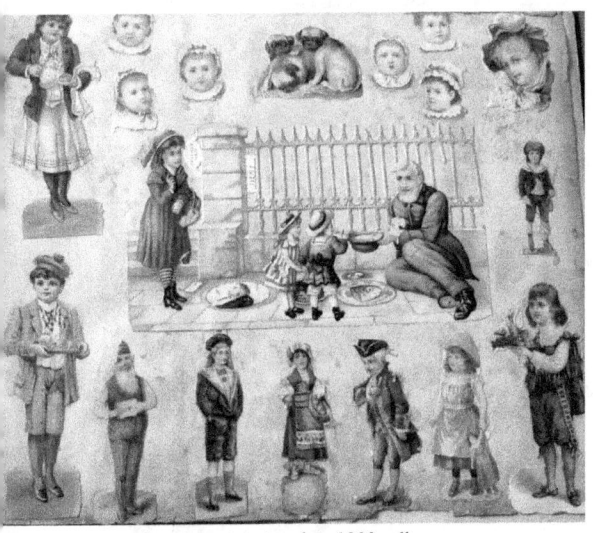

Scraps paste onto a late 1800s album page.

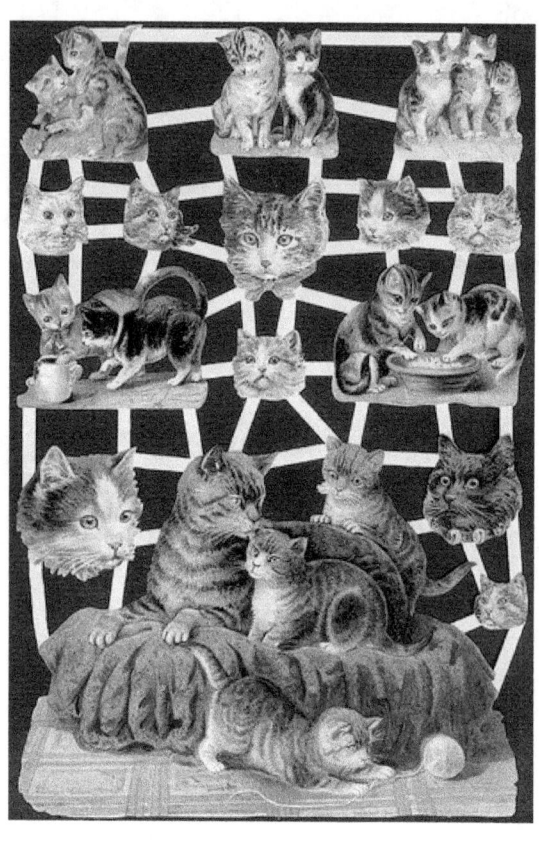

A sheet of cat scraps as they were sold, with all the pieces attached by tabs.

The limitations of electronic diamond testers

You can buy inexpensive electronic diamond detectors at places like amazon.com and eBay. They are useful devises and work by testing the material properties of a substance. They do, however, have a basic limitation: they can tell the difference between diamonds and simulant diamonds, but not between synthetic diamonds and natural diamonds.

Simulant diamonds are non-diamond materials like quartz, leaded glass and cubic zirconium that can superficially resemble diamonds. The electronic diamond detector identifies these as simulants as the have different material properties than real diamonds.

Synthetic diamonds, on the other hand, are genuine diamonds, but they're human made in a lab rather than geologically over time by nature. Synthetic and natural diamonds share the same material properties and the electronic diamond detector can't tell them apart. To the detector, they're both diamond.

Synthetic diamonds for jewelry are a recent phenomenon, so a electronic pocket detector will tell you if your great grandma's untouched wedding ring has a genuine natural diamond. There weren't any synthetic diamonds in 1885.

But in other circumstances, especially with modern jewelry and items purchased without certification or from sellers you don't know, the detector can only tell that it is diamond, not synthetic or natural.

Silver baseball buckle

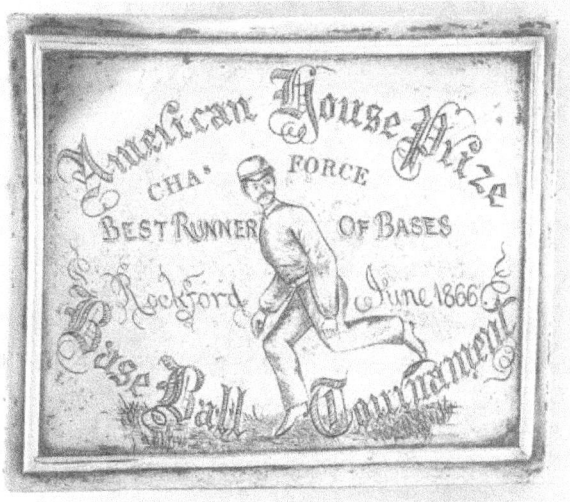

The above pictures a unique engraved solid silver belt buckled awarded to a Chas. Force in 1866 Rockford Illinois for winning a contest at a baseball tournament. In the early days of baseball, uniforms were rather generic and teams were identified by their colorful belts and belt buckles. A belt buckle as award was a natural choice.

Early counterfeit protection

To prevent counterfeiting, master printmaker Albrecht Durer made his prints so detailed and intricate that no one else had to ability to copy them. Shown here is one of his woodcut prints.

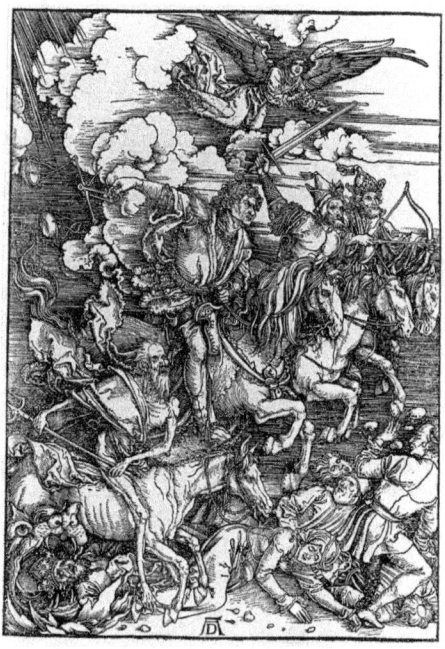

Original by artist?

An original work of art by a famous artist is an original that was made or, at times, closely supervised by the artist.

While artists often have assistants who help out, and the printing of a lithograph or forging of a metal sculpture may be a two or three person job, an original by an artist can't have been made without Picasso's approval or awareness.

There will be debates about how involved an artist was in the making of a particular print. If the artist 'telephoned it in' and his assistants did most of the work, many collectors will not consider the work an original of the artist, or at least entirely by the artist.

❧

The Illusion of Depth in Two Dimensional Art

Creating the perception of depth in paintings, sketches and photographs is a challenge, one that cannot be completely solved. This is because depth is three dimensional, while a sketch, photographic print or painting is two dimensional. Three dimensions cannot physically exist in two dimensions— they are mutually exclusive.

Over the centuries artists have developed techniques to create the superficial representation of depth in 2D art. Before these techniques, paintings and sketches lacked any sense of depth. Cave drawings appear primitive as the artists didn't understand the standard concepts of depicting depth. An early European painting shows objects in unreal proportions to each other. A mile away person may be the same size as a person up close. People today would compare the proportions to 'kid's drawings.'

The following shows just a few standard techniques used to give paintings, sketches and other 2D art the illusion of depth. These are techniques you can observe in art at the museum. These are also 'techniques' you can observe in a real life, such as when looking at your living room or across your back yard.

After all, the art is attempting to duplicate natural scenes like these.

Overlapping objects

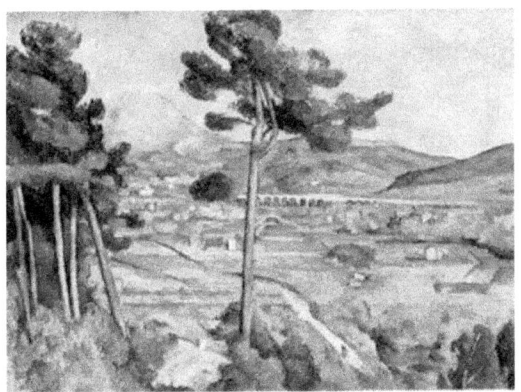

An object appears to be in front of the object(s) it overlaps. Overlapping is the strongest indicator of relative distance, overriding all other signs when there is seeming conflict. In the above Cezanne painting, the large center tree overlaps the *distant* bridge, mountain and sky.

Diminishing scale

With things that are believed to be of same or similar size (2 cats or 2 basketballs), the visually larger appears to be closer than the smaller. In the Cezanne painting, the viewer assumes that the tree is much smaller than the distant hills. Thus the difference in scale (tree taking up more painting space than the hills) makes it appear as if the tree is closer.

Diagonal lines representing diminishing scale

An exemplification of diminishing scale, diagonal lines moving towards each other as they move up or down a painting or sketch give the illusion of depth. A real world example of this is a straight road that appears to become skinnier as it approaches the distant horizon. Another example is when you stand at one end of an empty hallway and watch the lines where the wall and floor meet visually move towards each other as they move to the farther side of the room.

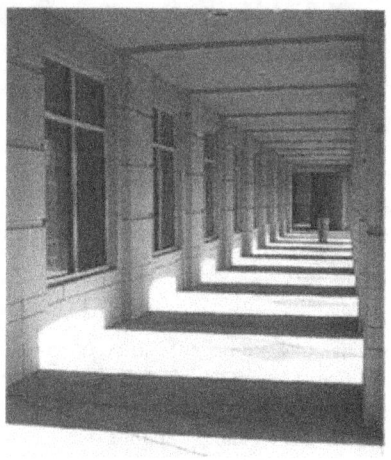

This photo shows diagonal

Focus

Things that are in focus tend to be perceived as closer than things that are out of focus. This makes sense, as a road sign is blurry if too far away.

Similarly, objects that have more intense color, detail and contrast often appear closer than objects that are blurrier, hazier and less focused.

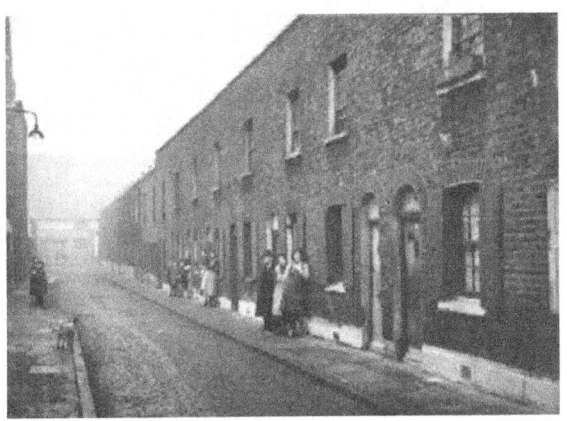

In this old photograph depth is shown by diminishing scale, the narrowing lines of the road and building tops, and that with distance things become blurrier and hazier.

A problem in trying to create realistic depth in two dimensions is that the human is designed to detect real depth not a flat representation.

Looking at the real back yard, each eye looks at the 3D objects from a different angle, the head and body movement creating even more perspectives. The mind combines these different views into the mind's image.

This cannot be done with a two dimensional object. With a still life painting, and even a still life photograph, it is not possible for the eyes to get the different views of the fruit bowl that is needed to perceive a truly 3D fruit bowl. The photograph, no matter how clear, shows only one angle.

Notice that many attempts to create a closer to true 3D effect involve alteration not just to the flat image but of the viewer's vision. 3D movies and pictures often require special glasses and viewers.

Chinese antique exports

In order to protect its national cultural heritage, it is illegal in China since 2009 to export any Pre-1900 Chinese antiques. Assume any vase, work of art or other artifact sold directly from China is from after 1900. It is, however, legal to export from China Chinese items from 1900 and after and these items sometime come with red export seals. The seal is not authentication of the item, just marking that a government inspector deemed the item not to be Pre-20th century and it was exported legally.

Wirephotos: 'Overnight photos'

In the early 1900s, there was no overnight national distribution of images. Photographs were shipped by plane, train and even boat. While this was okay for the many popular monthly magazines, most early daily. newspapers had relatively few and dated images

While turn of the century news services could send the printed text of a story via telephone lines ('wire') to subscribing newspapers, they also wanted to be able send photographs in a similar way. Originally, this was just a pipe dream. Even today the idea of sending photographs over the telephone sounds incredible. The invention of the wirephoto process eventually led to overnight photograph distribution.

The wirephoto process allowed photographs to be transferred through telephone lines. The process required a large, expensive wirephoto machine both at the source and at the receiving end. The original photograph was placed inside the wirephoto machine. Much like today's computer scanner, an electronic eye scanned the photograph and translated it into electrical impulses. These impulses were sent through the telephone wire to the identical wirephoto machine at the receiving end. At the receiving machine the impulses were translated to light that was used to develop the image onto photographic paper. The development would take minutes to over an hour, as the photographic paper was slowly exposed line by line. In fact, the ultimate way to identify the wirephoto (the received image) is to look for the tiny horizontal or vertical lines in the image.

The result was that that the receiving newspaper had a copy of the original photograph that it could use to make prints for the newspaper. This wirephoto had an identical image to the original photograph, but of lesser quality.

A wirephoto could be sent simultaneously to many receivers. The Associated Press could put the original photograph into the wirephoto machine and send copies to the Seattle Times, New York Times, San Francisco Chronicle and Green Bay Press-Gazette all at once. The Associated Press' main office in New York City could send wirephotos to its regional office in Atlanta, and the Atlanta office could send wirephotos to the New York City office. As you can imagine, this made photograph distribution quicker and more efficient than transporting a box of photos by train.

While the wirephoto process was invented in 1921, and AT & T had its first commercial wirephoto service in 1925, it took at least a decade for the process to be used widely. The early machines were large, overly expensive and the process unreliable. The early wirephotos were usually of poor quality and hostage to the fickleness and 'breaks' of the telephone lines.

When someone sent a wirephoto across the telephone lines, it often took more than an hour and the sender had no idea if a recognizable image would be received at the other end. Before 1935, wirephotos were only used for especially important, breaking news. In 1934 Associated Press (AP), the world's largest news service, installed an advanced and effective wirephoto system. Starting the following year, the wirephoto system became practical. Soon after other major news services installed their own wirephoto systems. This included AP's rivals International News Photos, United Press Association and ACME News pictures.

Though press photos were still distributed the old fashioned way, and a newspaper and magazine still hired its own photographers, the wirephoto system was the dominant form of international photo distribution from 1935 until the mid 1970s.

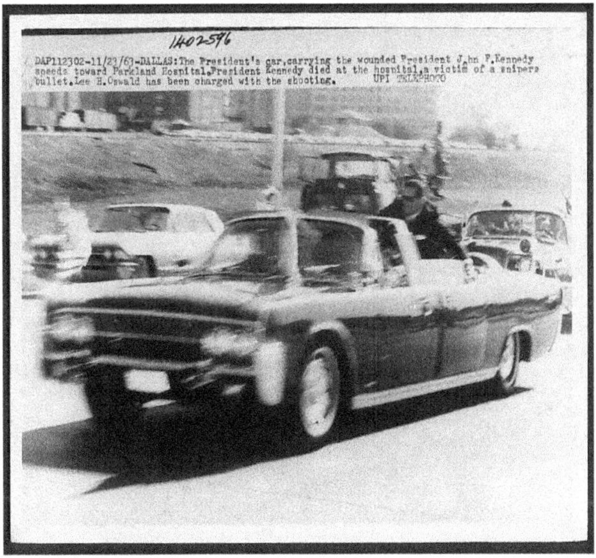
1402596
DAP112302-11/23/63-DALLAS:The President's car,carrying the wounded President John F.Kennedy speeds toward Parkland Hospital.President Kennedy died at the hospital,a victim of a snipers bullet.Lee H.Oswald has been charged with the shooting.
UPI TELEPHOTO

1963 wirephoto showing timely news: John F Kennedy being raced to a Dallas hospital after being shot. The upper border has the caption.

❧
Op Art

Op Art, short for optical art, is a form of art that uses lines, forms and patterns to trick the eye into perceiving nonexistent movement or other optical illusions. The art plays shows the ambiguity and margin of error in our perception.

Staring at the following two examples, you will variously see pulsating, shifting and rotating movement where there is one. You own eyes aren't always reliable.

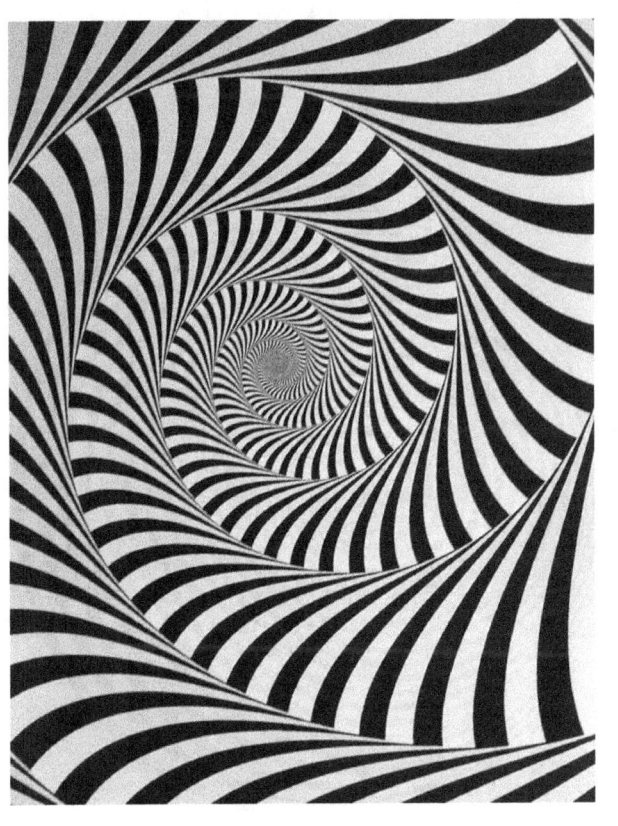

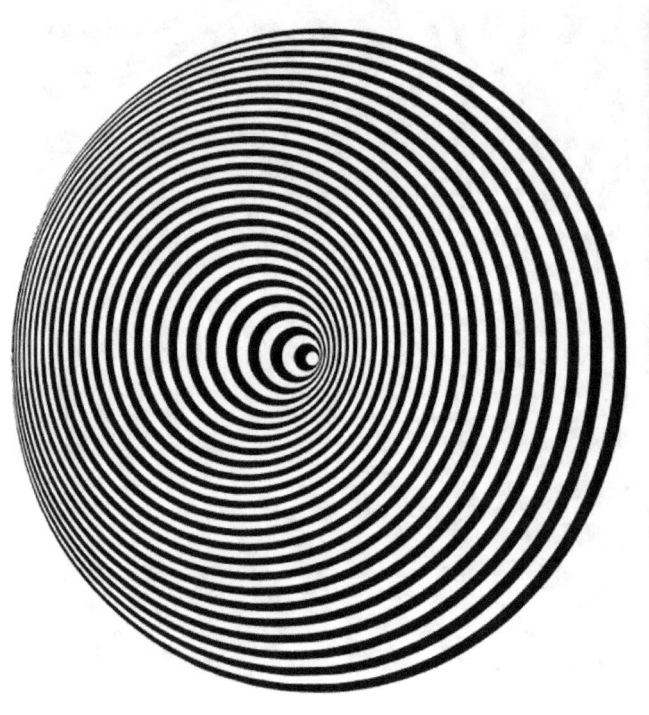

Symbols

Symbols are an integral part of the human experience on many levels. A symbol is something that represents something else, something larger. It is a shorthand, often to a complex idea. To many a cross symbolizes Jesus Christ and represents Christianity. A gold ring on the finger symbolizes marriage. Shadows in a movie can symbolize danger and mystery.

Not only can commonly known symbols be used in art to communicate ideas, meaning and mood, but this illustrates how humans don't need reality to communicate real ideas. Symbols literally aren't the thing they symbolize.

Literature, this very page you are reading, is a long series of symbols. The meaning isn't in the symbols themselves, but what they represent and evoke in your mind. I couldn't communicate many of the ideas in this book to you without these symbols.

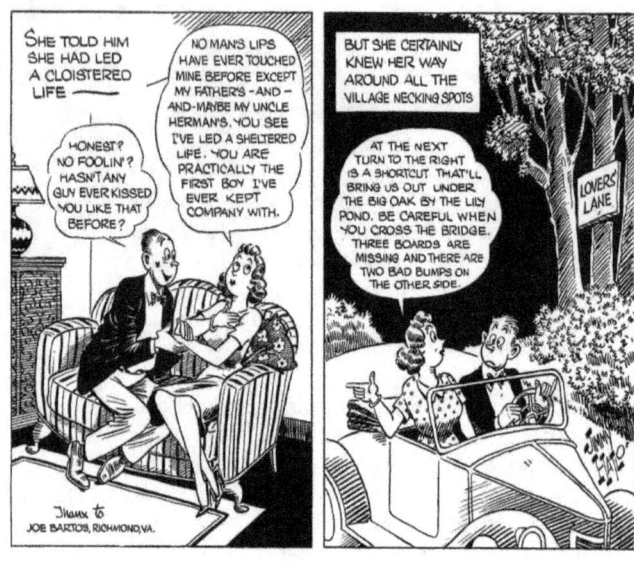

This comic strip uses a plethora of artificial symbols to communicate to the readers. There are symbols of people, bubbled words to indicate speaking, and panels to represent the passage of time.

Aleatory Art

> "Any path is right, if— as according to
> Bach-- it leads to the divine"
> — music historian Paul Epstein on
> J.S. Bach's fugues, to which Bach never
> gave a playing order.

Aleatory art is art where the finished result is
substantially out of the artist's hands. It can
involve chance or the musician's or audience's
choice. Many games are aleatory. Monopoly
involves the roll of the dice. Poker involves the
shuffling of the cards. Aleatory in art can create
fresh, inventive, unexpected results. If the
results defies the conventions of plot, narrative
and order, that's the point.

J.S. Bach's little fugues are aleatory in
that he never communicated which order the
short musical pieces should be played. They
can be played or listened to in any order, take
your pick, randomly program the CD player. In
the above quote, Epstein is saying an overall
sublime aesthetic result justifies whichever
fugue order lead to it. It's reminiscent of the
Hindu saying, "Any path that leads to God is
correct."

Novelist William S. Burroughs used the
so called cut-up aleatory technique. Pages of
text were physically cut up and randomly

pieced back together, sometimes with text by other authors, creating new and often profoundly surreal meaning and narrative. Burroughs believed this type of collage more closely represented the human experience. Despite the conceit of linearity, humans don't think or experience things linearly, one's thoughts constantly flipping back and forth between past, current and future. Random little events and objects trigger memories and provoke speculation of the future. When you consider buying a can of beans in the grocery aisle, you think about past meals and the future meal where these beans might be used. The human ability to identify flowers, shoe brands and people involves comparing the present to memory. Human intelligence and reasoning involves mentally flipping back and forth through time.

Even with a physically bound paper book, the reader chooses the order in which the book is read. Whether or not they realize it, readers are as responsible for the order as the author, though the author usually gets the blame.

William S. Burroughs said the chapters of his novel *Naked Lunch* could be read in any order. That a reader read them 1, 2, 3 had nothing to do with him.

❧

Nearly all existing Ancient Greek paintings are on pottery. The Ancient Greeks are better known for their sculpture and architecture.

Ancient Roman painting is much more plentiful than the ancient Greeks. As the Romans often emulated the Greaks, art historians use Roman art to study Greek art.

Manipulative Gum Companies
a Rare Baseball Card

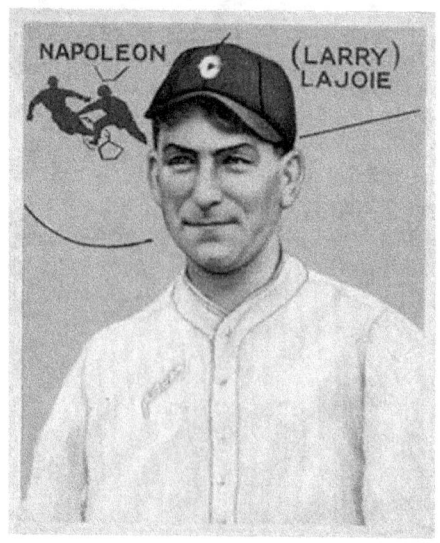

Though its value has fallen a bit in recent years, the pictured 1933 Goudey #106 Napoleon Lajoie has traditionally been one of the most coveted baseball cards due to its rarity. It was produced during the American depression as part of a colorful 240 card set by The Goudey Gum Company, a Boston manufacturer of chewing gum. As with most 'bubblegum cards' marketed to kids these baseballs cards were included in small wax paper wrapped packs with a stick or two of gum.

As a ploy to move their product, Goudey intentionally didn't print card #106, the one shown here and depicting Hall of Fame player Lajoie. The reason was the collecting habit of kids back then was to finish a set, meaning collect one of each different card #1 thru #240. With #106 nonexistent, kids kept on buying packs in a futile attempt to finish their sets.

A number of disappointed kids went as far to write Goudey to complain they couldn't find the card #106. Goudey relented, printed up a small number #106 cards and mailed them only to the kids who wrote. Some of the 1933 Goudey #106 Napoleon Lajoies can be found with the original paperclip mark from how they were mailed to the kids.

And you thought the Lajoie was tough

Even rarer than the Goudey Napoleon Lajoie,
and for similar reason rare, is the 1923 Maple
Crispette #15 baseball card. Maple Crispette
was a Canadian candy and the cards were sold
in packs of the candy. As described on the
cards backs, a complete set could be redeemed
for a baseball, bat or a glove. To make the
redemptions difficult and to sell more candy,
card #15 of Casey Stengel was made almost
non existent. Today only one example of the
Stengel card is known to exist.

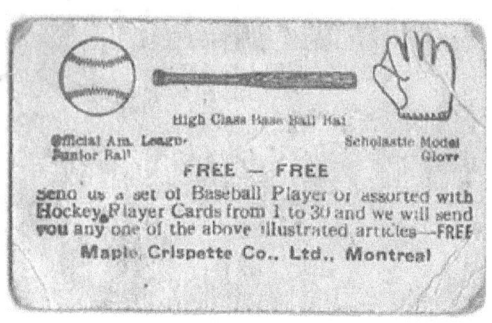

Using a black light to identify many fakes

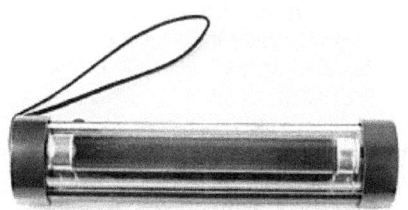

An inexpensive and easy to use longwave black light is great tool for quickly identifying reprints and fakes of Pre World War II paper material. This includes trading cards, photographs, programs, books posters, postcards, tickets and anything made of paper.

A black light is effective in identifying many, though not all, modern paper stocks.

Starting in the late 1940s, manufacturers of many products began adding optical brighteners and other new chemicals to their products. Optical brighteners are invisible dyes that fluoresce brightly under ultraviolet light. They were used to make products appear brighter in normal daylight, which contains some ultraviolet light. Optical brighteners were added to laundry detergent and clothes to help disguise and to give the often advertised `whiter than white whites.' Optical brighteners were added to plastic toys to makes them brighter and more colorful. Paper manufacturers joined the act as well, adding optical brighteners to many, though not all of their white papers stocks.

A black light can identify many trading cards, posters, photos and other paper items that contain optical brighteners. In a dark room and under black light optical brighteners will usually fluoresce a very bright light blue or bright white. To find out what this looks like shine a recently made white trading card, snapshot or most types of today's printing paper under a black light.

If paper stock fluoresces very bright as just described, it almost certainly was made after the mid 1940s.

It is important to note that not all modern papers will fluoresce this way, as optical brighteners are not added to all modern paper. For example, many modern wirephotos have no optical brighteners. This means that if a paper doesn't fluoresce brightly this does not mean it is necessarily old. However, with few exceptions, if a paper object fluoresces very brightly, it could not have been made before World War II. It is important that the collector gain practical experience. This means using a black light to examine and compare the fluorescence of a variety of items. With photographs, make sure you shine the black light on all sides and edges. This is because the gelatin or other coating on the front of the paper often prevents the front from fluorescing.

The beauty of this black light test is you can use it on items you aren't an expert on. You may be no expert on 1920s German Expressionist movie posters or 1890s Canadian fishing industry pamphlets, but you can still identify many modern reprints.

The Ambiguity of Language

Even in Kyoto how I long for Kyoto when the cuckoo sings
  – Matsuo Basho (1644-1694)

Our daily spoken and written language is ambiguous and can be interpreted in different ways. Words often have multiple meaning, phrases can be interpreted in different ways, much meaning is implied rather than spelled out. A listener's or reader's interpretation of the ambiguous language is guided by many things including experience, habit, assumptions and educated guess, culture, expectations.

  "John and I went to the food court. We
  ate at the Taste of India."

The preceding everyday sentence seems straight foreward but can be interpreted in many different logical ways. The 'we' of the second sentence commonly is read to mean John and 'I,' but this is an assumption. It could mean the narrator and someone other than John, or perhaps the narrator, John and someone else or multiple people. It's very much plausible they caught up with someone else on the way to the Taste of India. The sentence is not explicit in what 'we' means, even if we initially think it is.

We read the sentence to mean the Taste of India is at the food court, and they ate there soon after they arrived there. However, this is just a guess, if a guess based on experience. There's nothing in the sentence that says the Taste of India isn't far away from the food court and their eating didn't take place days if not months later.

* * * *

The ambiguity and varying interpretations of language often has comic effect, such as in the following two clips from the movie Naked Gun 1-1/2.

Lt. Frank Drebin: Miss, I'm Lt. Frank Drebin, and this is Captain Ed Hocken, Police Squad.

Shapely Female Shop Assistant: Is this some kind of bust?

Lt. Frank Drebin: Well... it's very impressive, yes, but we need to ask you a few questions.

Lt. Frank Drebin: Now, Jane, what can you tell us about the man you saw last night?

Jane: He's Caucasian.

Ed: Caucasian?

Jane: Yeah, you know, a white guy. A mustache. About six-foot-three.

Lt. Frank Drebin: Awfully big mustache.

* * * *

In the earlier Matsuo Basho 'can't go home again' haiku, the word Kyoto was has two meanings. The first and second Kyotos mean two things. Or, at least that's how it's interpreted.

People assume that the double entendre was intentional by Basho, but we don't know. Our assumptions about Basho's intent are just assumptions.

The Difference Between
a Fake a Forgery

A forgery is an item that was made to fool others into believing it is something it is not. This includes counterfeits, but also made up items like a 'newly discovered' Rembrandt painting.

On the other hand, a fake is an item that is seriously misidentified. This includes forgeries and counterfeits. It also includes items that are innocently misidentified by collectors or sellers who are uninformed.

When in doubt about seller or maker's intent, it's best to call a bad sale or auction item a fake instead of a forgery or counterfeit. All three words mean an item is not genuine, but forgery and counterfeit implies intentional illegality.

Islamic Art

By Islamic belief, artwork is flawed compared to the work of God. It is thought that attempting to depict the realistic form of an animal or person is religious heresy. Thus Islamic art generally, but not always, lacks realistic humans and animals, and is noted instead for its intricate and elaborate patterns and designs.

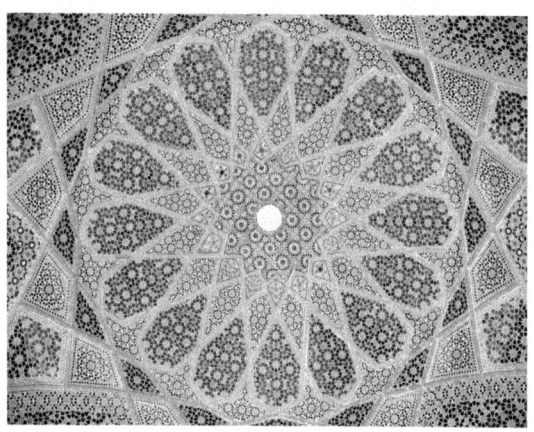

Law and Expert Opinion

Due to the real or perceived litigious nature of some art owners, many scholars and experts have become reluctant to give their opinions about the authenticity of a work of art. In years before, open authenticity discussions about art was normal and encouraged, but scholars have been sued over their opinions. Even when the scholar is correct and and the court agrees, the court costs can be prohibitive. The Andy Warhol Foundations for the Visual Arts and Roy Lichtenstein Foundations discontinued their authentication boards due the potential of lawsuits and liability insurance. Though the Warhol Foundation won a lawsuit brought by a collector, the legal costs were $7 million.

In some cases, the authenticity is legally decided by a judge or jury. This of course brings up the topic of art authenticity being decided by judges and juries who are not art experts. And the art market doesn't have to agree with the verdict. A work of art a judge decides is authentic, may not sell well at auction as collectors find it suspect.

A common misconception
about limited editions

Some prints, photographs and other types of art and collectibles are limited edition numbered: say, 1/50 (1 of 50 made), 2/50, 3/50 .... 50/50. Some collectors feel that the first print or photograph or figurine 'off the presses,' is the most valuable, and, as one might expect, pick one that is numbered 1/50. The thing they don't realize is that the works are rarely numbered in the order of printing. The numbering and signing was often done well after the printing or manufacture. For example, Marc Chagall would go through the stack of prints, picking out which ones he liked and sign and hand numbering the ones that met his approval. He wasn't trying to keep things in order of printing. Thus, the print numbered 1/50 may or may not have been first one off the printing press. Print # 12/50 or 6/50 may have been the first. And there's no way to know for sure.

Illusion in movie watching

Despite audience perception, movies don't show continuous, real movement of a deer running, a car racing or people conversing, but a series of snapshots of the movement. If you hold up old movie film, you will see it is a series of still images lined up side by side, not unlike the panels in a newspaper comic strip. When the film is shot and shown at the proper speed, the viewer's mind incorrectly interprets the succession of still images as real movement. To the mind, 'realistic movement' seems the most plausible explanation for what it is seeing. This choice is made instantly and nonconsciously and the viewer simply thinks she's watching real, continuous movement.

How do you know if one of those big John
James Audubon bird prints is original?

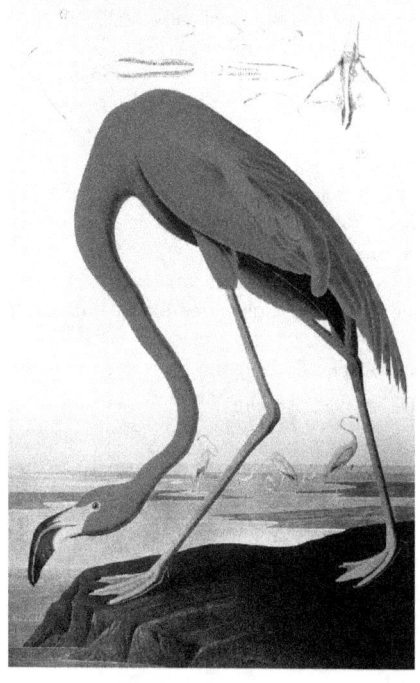

The wildly popular large Audubon "Birds of America" prints were originally printed in the 1820s-30s, and have been reprinted many times since, including as cheap posters. Luckily for collectors, identifying the original large prints is surprisingly easy if you know what to look for.

An original large 1820s-30s Audubon "Birds of America" print should have the following four qualities (There are also genuine small (1/8th) size Audubon prints, but this brief essay is only about the jumbo versions):

1) The original prints should measure about 26x39 inches if untrimmed. A reprint can be the same size, but an untrimmed odd size is a giveaway a print is a later reprint.

2) Look for a "J Whatman" watermark in the paper. A watermark is best seen when holding the paper up in front of a bright light. Many of today's computer printer and typing papers have watermarks, so you can practice your looking skills on paper around the house. The Audubon watermarks will say J Whatman and a year of printing below (ala '1831').

It's possible that if the watermark was at the very edge of the paper and the print was trimmed that the watermark may be missing or obscured. For the potential buyer it's best to make sure that whole watermark is in the paper, and leave the "was trimmed off" watermarks for other buyers.

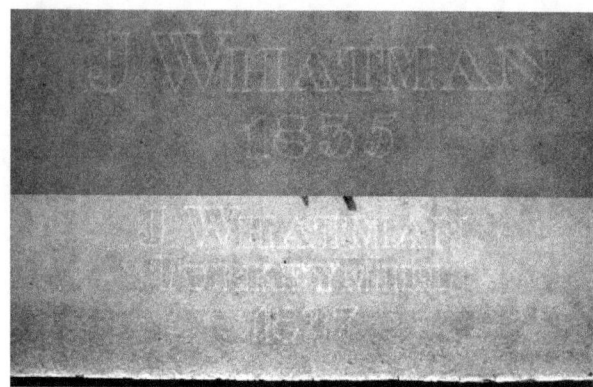

1835 J. Whatman watermark

3) Presence of a plate mark. A plate mark is an indentation in the paper that surrounds the printed graphics. Caused by the pressure from the metal printing plate against the paper during printing, it appears only with certain types of printing techniques. Some reproductions might have fake plate marks, but most will have none.

4) Hand painted colors. The colors on the original large Audubons were painted by hand. Under close examination, this will be apparent. If under a strong magnifying glass, the colors have a fine multicolor dot pattern as on a magazine picture, it's a later photomechanical reproduction. A small few of reproductions have hand painted colors, but the majority of modern reprints will have the multi-color dot pattern.

If a print has all of the above qualities, it is near certain that you have an original on your hands. The watermark, in particular, is a strong sign of originality, as it doesn't appear on any known reprint sets. As a reproduction can be hand colored, be of the correct size or have a plate mark, remember to check all four qualities and don't focus on just one.

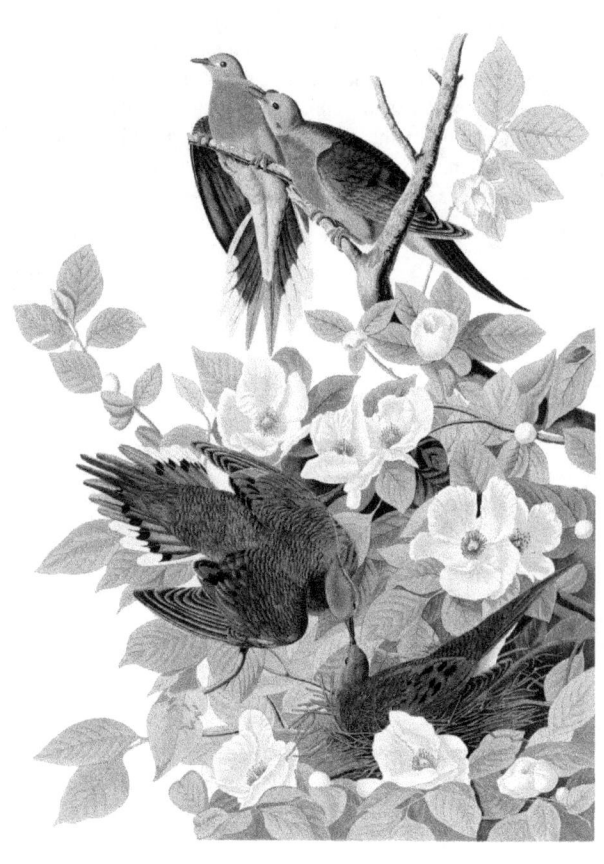

Audubon

≈

Early forms of money

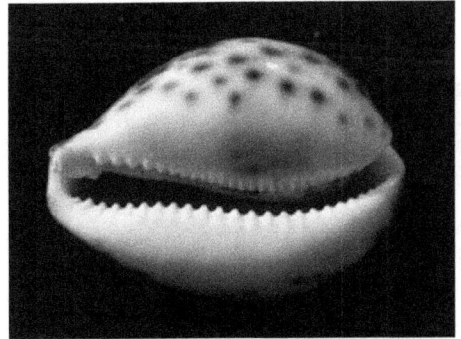

cowrie, an early form of money

Money has taken many material forms over the years. Cows, sheep and goats were first used as currency thousands of years before Jesus Christ. Grains were also an early currency.

Cowries, the shells of a molluscs, were a popular form of currency for any years, including in China.

Bronze and copper cowrie imitations were manufactured by China at the end of the Stone Age and can be considered some of the earliest forms of metal coins.

Metal tool money, such as knife and spade shaped monies, was also used in China. These were also precursors of modern metal coins .

The Chinese also used leather strips with text on them as money, moving close to the first paper bills.

American Indians used wampum,which were strings of beads.

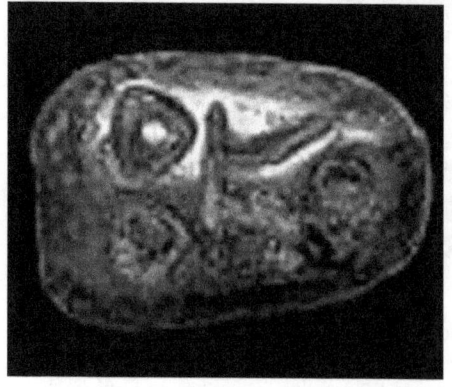

Metal cowrie

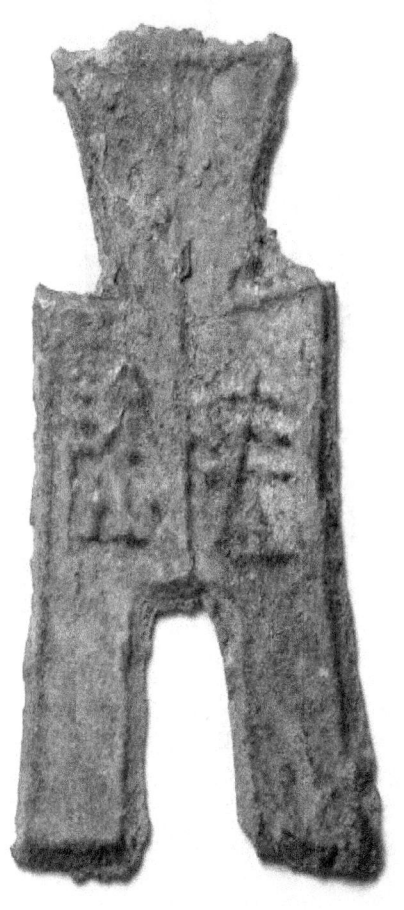

early Chinese spade coin

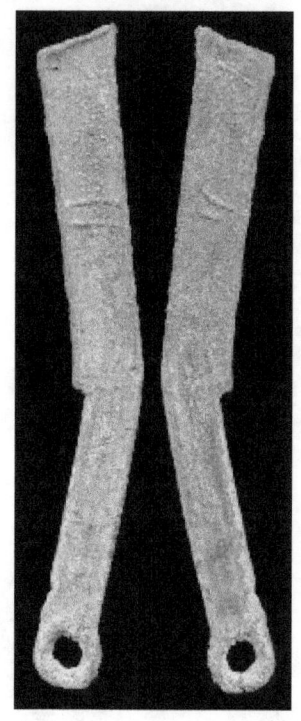

Early Chinese knife coins

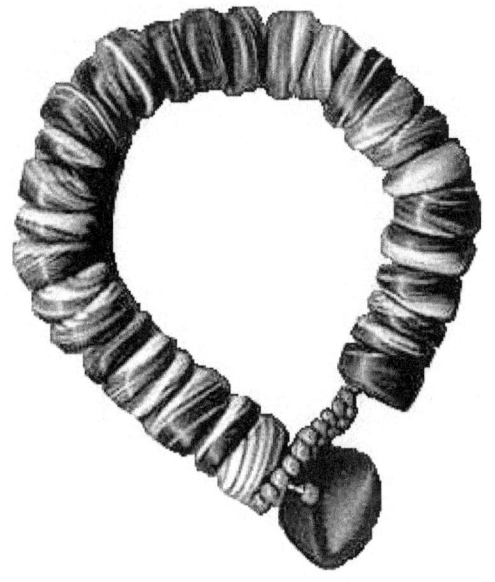

American Indian wampum

Hand signing a print is a relatively recent thing, starting in the late 1800s. Original Rembrandt and Albrecht Durer prints are not hand signed. Durer prints often have his machine printed monogram as part of the printed graphics.

In modern times, the artist's hand signature on an original print shows that the print was personally approved as finished by the artist. The artist signs it when it's all finished and meets his or her approval. Prints that didn't come out right go unsigned and are often literally destroyed and tossed in the trash. This explains why art collectors pay more for a hand signed original print by a famous artist. The extra price is not just because it's autographed, but because the autographed indicates the print was personally okayed by the artist.

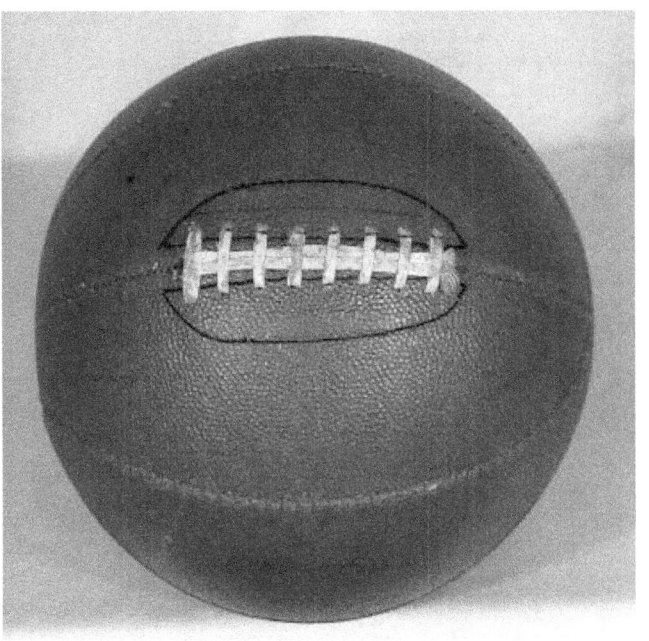

Early basketballs were laced giving them an unpredictable bounce. This meant there was more passing and less dribbling in the game.

Action painting is a style of painting in which paint is spontaneously dribbled, splashed or smeared onto the canvas, rather than being carefully applied. The resulting work often emphasizes the physical act of painting itself as an essential aspect of the finished work. Jackson Pollock most is the most famous action painter.

X-Rays in Art Authentication

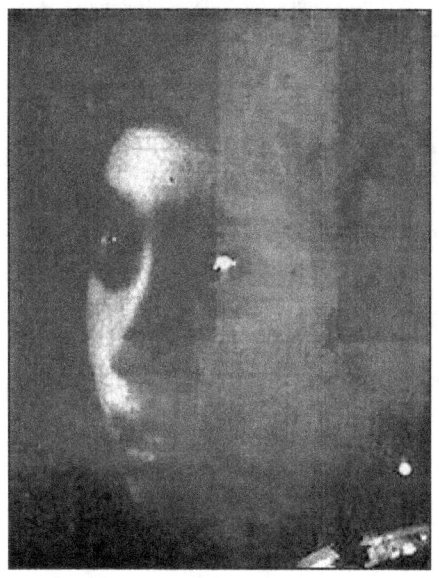

X-ray machines are used to examine paintings in much the way they are used to examine human bodies.

As with ultraviolet and infrared light, X-rays are a form of light invisible to human eyes. X-rays pass straight through some materials, but are reflected or absorbed by others. In the physician's office, the X-ray machine shoots X-rays at the patient and has X-ray sensitive photographic film on the other the other side of the patient. Duly note that 'film' is an old fashioned term and technology as even X-ray machines have hit the digital age. The X-rays pass through the patient's skin and flesh and go to the film, but are absorbed by the bones. The result is the X-ray photograph shows the inside bones, allowing the doctor to examine the inside of the body.

Art historians get a similar insides look at paintings, as X-rays go through some paints but are absorbed or reflected by others. The picture shows an X-ray photograph of Jan Vermeer's iconic 17th century 'Girl with a Pearl Earring.' The white paint on her face and the pearl show up due to a period metal in the paint.

This helps the historian in two ways. First, the identification of certain materials can date the paint and painting. Second, it often shows what was painted underneath the first level graphics we see with our naked eyes. Famous artists are known to have had standard ways and personal styles in how they constructed their paintings, which help the historian in judging the authenticity, and some paintings started out as dramatically different designs. X-rays have shown that Picasso's famous 'The Old Guitar Player' started off as an old woman instead of an old man, and an El Greco portrait started as a still life.

Microscopy in Authentication

A microscope is often used by an authentication expert to date the kind of printing used to make both photographs and ink-and-printing-press prints. Modern reprints and counterfeits are often identified because the microscope shows the printing is too modern. An 1870 print couldn't have been made with a printing technology invented in 1985.

For example, the following shows what 'elecrostatic' printing looks like under the 100X power microscope. Electrostatic printing is the modern technology used to make Xeroxes, photocopies and home computer laser print. Large numbers of reproductions of antique prints and photos have been made using this type of printing.

Under the microscope, the modern electrostatic prints are easily identified by the unique and quirky pattern of the pigment (dry ink). In this printing process the lines are made up of many tiny dust-like grains of pigment that have been fused (melted) to the paper. When you handle ink jet cartridges you will notice the pigment/ink is dusty and dry and can get all over the place if you are not careful. In the printing process not all the grains of pigment make it to the intended area before being fused, so the print is identified by the many stragglers outside the lines. It looks as if it needs a dusting.

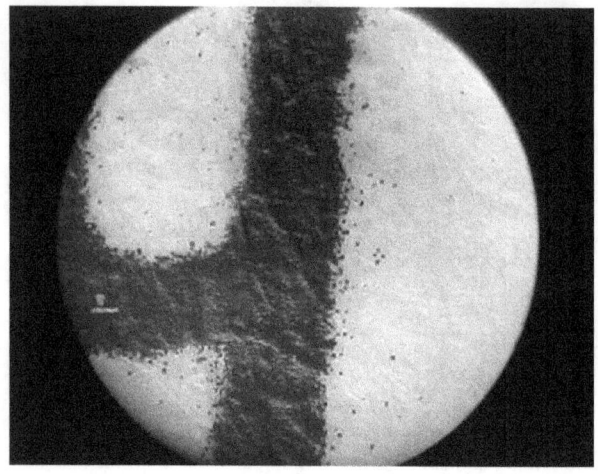

This image, and the distinct 'dusty' pigment pattern, would prove a so-called '19th century engraving' is a modern fake.

Ultramarine

In the Middle Ages West, the blue paint ultramarine was as valuable as gold. Ultramarine was considered a pure, divine color and was difficult to make. It was used with genuine gold and vermillion (a type of red) for important illustrated documents. In paintings, the robes of the Virgin Mary were ultramarine and people owned paintings with ultramarine to demonstrate their wealth.

The blue mineral for the paint came from the East, with the name ultramarine meaning 'beyond the sea.' Ultra means beyond and marine refers to the ocean.

❧

Triptych

A triptych painting is a painting comprised of three panels, each thematically related. They were traditionally made for religious purposes, painted on wood and hinged together so they could be closed, or folded together, a bit like a book.

Pictured is a famous circa 1500 triptych on oak by Hieronymus Bosch showing a Christian tale of Adam and Eve on left, a depraved sexual earth in the middle and the torments of Hell on right. Bosch is famed for his fantastical, highly detailed and often disturbing scenes filled with bizarre imagery and cryptic symbols. When the panels are closed, it shows Bosch's geographically-incorrect view of the world.

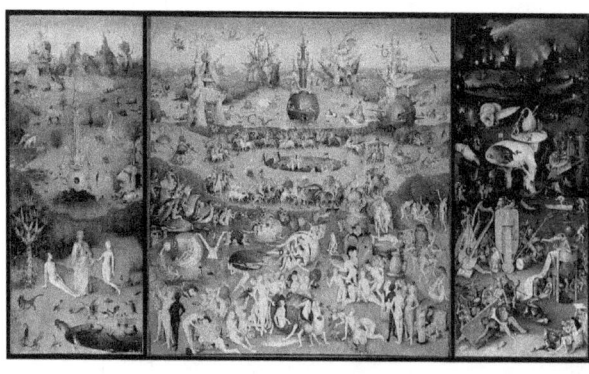

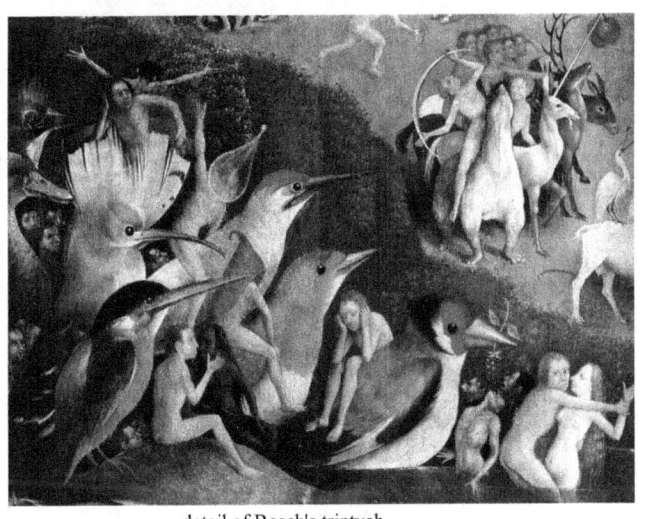

detail of Bosch's triptych

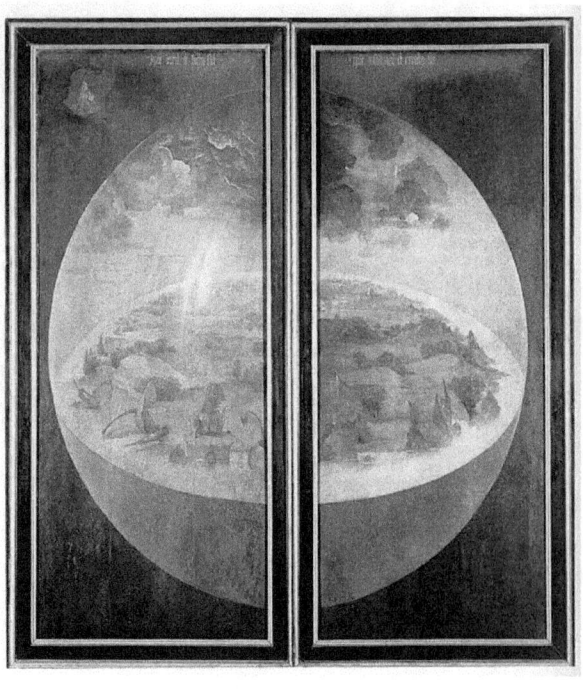

Bosch's triptych when closed, showing his
curious perception of the earth.

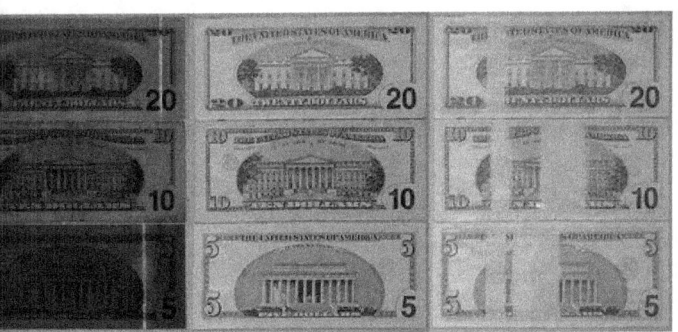

US currency is amongst the most advanced printed items in the world, containing special watermarks, imbedded hairs, expensive paper and invisible markers. This photo shows three columns of $20, $10 and $5 bills (left to right) under ultraviolet light, visible light and infrared light, revealing hidden lines, bars and markers. These markers help authenticate bills and identify forgeries.

Restoration

The value, desirability and even ethicalness of restoration is treated differently in different areas of collecting. For a famous old painting, restoration is often considered desirable and can even raise the market value. Similarly, restoration of vintage movie posters is a common and accepted practice, though many collectors prefer the unrestored versions. In the trading card hobby, however, even the slightest alteration to a card can ruin a card's market value and many collectors would call it unethical to alter a trading card in any way. What is acceptable procedure for a Rembrandt painting in the Louvre would horrify most trading card collectors if done to a trading card.

≪❦≫

Dali's bomb prints

Dali made prints from metal printing plates prepared in creative ways. To help create the design for one printing plate, he blew up a home made bomb in front of it.

Expressionism

Expression is a twentieth century art movement that depicts the world subjectively. It radically distorts physical reality to communicate moods and other psychological ideas. The artists intend to express emotional experiences and meaning rather than physical reality.

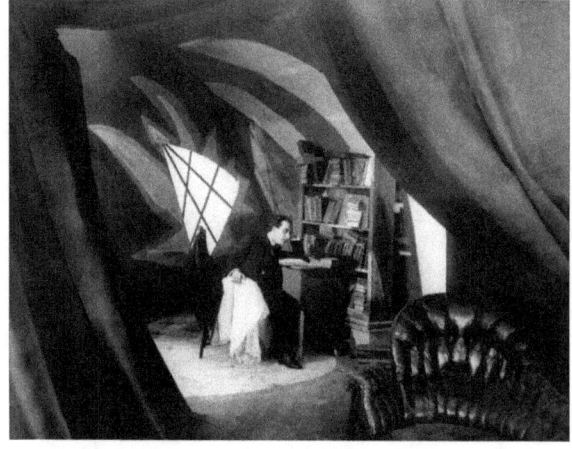

The 1920 silent German Expressionist movie Cabinet of Dr. Caligari used highly distorted sets to help convey the themes of insanity, dreams and evil.

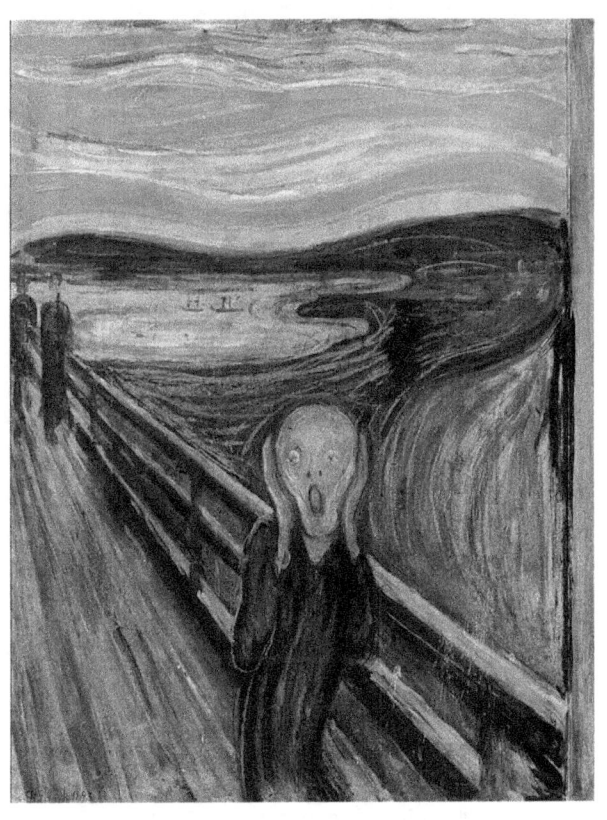

Perhaps the most famous expressionist work of art is Edvard Much's *The Scream*. It expresses an emotional meaning, not a physical reality.

"Can a home computer print be considered an original?"

Yes, if the design did not exist before--meaning it's not a reproduction or copy. Assuming there isn't major graphic embellishment, if someone scans and computer prints out the cover of Reader's Digest, that's not original. However, if your young daughter draws a unique picture of her kitty cat on a computer drawing program and prints it out for the refrigerator door, that's as original as that Rembrandt etching in the museum.

The common pitfall in defining what is original is assigning false qualities to the term. Common phrases one will hear include: "It's by Picasso and sold for $1 million. It's got to be original" . . . "A cheesy baseball card sold in packs of gum can't be as original as a painting" . . . " An original can't be in a kid's finger paints. It's got to be something like oils" . . . "I paid $1,000 for it, so I consider it an original" . . .

While financial value, artist's celebrity, beauty and prevailing taste are fine and dandy qualities, they have nothing to do with originality. The originality of your daughter's computer sketch isn't defined by its sell price on eBay.

David Cycleback is an art and artifact historian. His books include *Judging the Authenticity of Prints by the Masters; Judging the Authenticity of Photographs; Cognition, Perception and the Limits of Knowledge* and *Return Trip: Aesthetics and Epistemology.*